HOW TO CAPITALIZE ANYTHING

GIACOMO GIAMMATTEO

Inferno Publishing Company

Inferno Publishing Company

Houston, TX

For more information about this book visit my website.

Edition ISBNs

Trade Paperback 978-1-949074-49-9

E-book 978-0-9850302-9-2

Cover design by Natasha Brown

Book design by Giacomo Giammatteo

This edition was prepared by Giacomo Giammatteo
gg@giacomog.com

❀ Created with Vellum

CONTENTS

INTRODUCTION

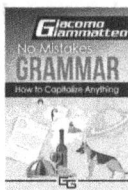

This book has one purpose: to address most of the capitalization issues we encounter today. Dictionaries don't come close to listing all the issues, and style guides offer generalized rules that are often vague and spread over a six-hundred-page book (or larger).

I once spent days—literally days—determining how to spell certain breed names for animals. It was necessary because both the CMOS (*Chicago Manual of Style*) and AP (*Associated Press*) style guides had rules they recommended, but then, in the examples given, they listed exceptions without explaining the reasoning behind those exceptions. And nowhere in those books were the reasons explained.

Both books also cited various rules for capitalizing geographic regions and terms using compass points, but again left a lot to be questioned—a whole lot.

These are just a few of the problems faced by millions every day. I hope to resolve many of those issues with this book. It won't solve all issues, but I think it will cover the majority of them, and the examples will be logically presented and include comprehensive index so you readily find whatever it is you're looking for.

The first chapter serves as an overview and covers a lot of different rules, but each chapter after that goes into more detail.

Style Guides

As a reminder, this book, as well as all style guides, is just that—a guide. These guides exist to provide a consistent way to stylize, format, capitalize, and punctuate words to make the process easier for both writers and readers. Read what CMOS has to say about it. The passage below is from their seventeenth edition.

CMOS can list only so many examples, and it's no good wasting time pondering fine distinctions, so if your document uses some terms that *Chicago* lowercases and others you aren't sure about, rather than agonize over possible inconsistencies, just look up the words in a dictionary. CMOS lowercases "french dressing" and "swiss cheese," but *Merriam-Webster's 11th Collegiate Dictionary* uppercases them (along with "Australian shepherd" and "German shepherd"). Make your choices with a mind to minimize inconsistencies, then record them on a style sheet.

You'll hear this throughout the book: select a style guide and dictionary, then stick with them. The style guide may be CMOS, AP, a guide used by the company you work for, or one you've created. Regardless of which one you decide on, stick with it. Don't follow CMOS for how it capitalizes animal breeds, then AP for how it deals with titles or geographic points.

My editor made a style guide for me. It was important because there are times I don't strictly follow any of the guides. She made this guide so that all my books would follow the same rules; in other words, if I used a comma in a certain way in book two, then the comma would be used the same way in book seventy. It's something to think about if you plan to write a lot. Speaking of which—the following is an example of what I just mentioned. It deals with how I handle italics versus quotation marks.

Before we start, I would like to touch on the way I use italics and quotation marks regarding words to be emphasized or words used as words.

If we're referring to a one-word example, I use italics. If more than one word, I wrap the words in quotes. There are a couple of exceptions made for consistency when both one-word and multiple-word examples occur within the same paragraph, as well as when words appear in a bulleted list.

By the way, throughout the book I use "different than" as opposed to "different from." I do this because I like it. When citing a comparative, I think *than* works better. Besides, most dictionaries and style guides have acknowledged that using *than* following *different* is not such a grievous sin.

One more note: Occasionally, I use *Chicago* instead of CMOS to indicate the *Chicago Manual of Style*. The reason is *Chicago* is changing the way it refers to itself because it caused confusion with some people in the computer industry, where CMOS means "complementary metal-oxide-semiconductor."

In future books and articles, I will use *Chicago* exclusively.

GENERAL CAPITALIZATION

Knowing when and when not to capitalize is an important part of writing. One thing that makes it difficult to master is the ever-changing rules, not to mention the disagreement between style guides and dictionaries. That's why it's important to select a style guide and dictionary you like, then stick with that decision.

This chapter is not intended to be a comprehensive source for all capitalization rules, covering all circumstances. It is meant to address the more common problems. For everything else, you should move to the chapter covering that topic or consult your favorite dictionary or style guide.

Without further ado, let's move on to the general rules.

Rule Number One

The first rule is simple:

- Start each sentence with a capital letter.

You wouldn't think so, but even this rule has exceptions.

There are a few words (usually brand names) that are spelled with the initial letters lowercased: iPhone, iPad, iCloud, iMac, eBay, etc.

The suggested way to deal with this is to rewrite the sentence so those words are not at the beginning; however, if you feel like the word should start the sentence, you may either capitalize it anyway or stick to the brand's suggested formatting and keep it lowercased:

- iPhones have become the best-selling phone of all time.
- According to Apple, iPhones have become the best-selling phones of all time.
- IPhones have become the best-selling phone of all time.

If it were me, I'd rewrite (example two). I don't like the lowercase *i* at the beginning of the sentence, nor do I like the look of *IPhone*. The spelling of *iPhone* with a lowercase *i* is so recognizable that the capitalized *I* looks odd.

Rule Number Two

Capitalize the names of family members, including nicknames.

- Uncle Ralph was one of my favorite uncles.

Both *uncle* and *Ralph* are capitalized because *uncle* is part of Ralph's name in this circumstance, but *uncles* (at the end of the sentence) is (not capitalized) A few more examples may help:

- "Mom, may I go to the mall?"

- "I went to the mall with Mom."
- "She's going to the mall with her mom."

In the first sentence, Mom is being addressed. In the second, *Mom* is a substitute for her name (whatever that may be), and in the third, neither of those situations apply. We're simply referring to her mom.

If you use a personal pronoun with a person's nickname, it doesn't require capitalization unless that nickname is being used as part of the person's name:

- my mom
- Mom
- her uncle
- her Uncle Ralph
- his aunt
- his Aunt Sally

Rule Number Three

Capitalize titles when part of a name (preceding the name, not coming after it)

☑ Senator Ted Ingles did not attend the rally.

☑ Ted Ingles, senator from Texas, did not attend the rally.

✗ Ted Ingles, Senator from Texas, did not attend the rally.

Rule Number Four

Do not capitalize a title if it is used as a general reference without the name.

☑ The president will not be coming tonight.

✗ The President will not be coming tonight.

Some style guides make allowances if *president* is being used to refer to the U.S. president, but not others.

- The president of Google just retired.
- Zimbabwe's president lands at Dulles airport tomorrow.

Rule Number Five
Capitalize a title when used in direct address:
☑ It's nice to meet you, Congressman.
☑ Senator, how nice to meet you.
✗ May I see you privately, detective?
☑ May I see you privately, Detective?
Rule Number Six
Capitalize proper nouns as well as adjectives derived from proper nouns:

- The Statue of Liberty
- The Brooklyn Bridge
- Italy
- San Francisco
- The King James Bible

The list of proper nouns is extensive and includes the names of people, specific places, companies, days of the week, months, man-made structures with names, specific geographic locations, cities, states, provinces, countries, islands, celestial bodies, works of art, museums, streets and roads, religions, names of deities, ethnicities, etc. Some examples follow:

- Washington Monument

- Mount Rushmore
- Mars (but not moon or sun)
- Venus (but not moon or sun)
- Baynard Boulevard
- Kansas
- Austin
- Africa
- Sicily
- East Coast
- the Hamptons (some people capitalize the word *the* before the name, but it should be lowercased.)
- the Atlantic Ocean
- the Amazon River
- Lake Superior
- The Hague (one of the few instances where *the* is capitalized)
- Apple
- Microsoft
- the Baltic Sea
- World War II
- the Constitution
- Napoleon
- Friday
- January
- *Houston Chronicle*
- Pittsburgh Penguins
- Texas Rangers
- Coca-Cola
- Congress
- Hinduism
- Buddha
- Bible

- Caucasian
- Oriental

I listed "The Hamptons" and "the Atlantic Ocean" and many others preceded by *the*.

Even though the article *the* frequently, if not always, precedes the proper noun, it is seldom capitalized. "The Hague" is one of the only examples I can think of when the article is capitalized related to a place-name.

The list goes on and on. One exception to the rule mentioned earlier regarding titles is this:

if a title is mentioned and that title refers to a specific high-ranking executive of the government—and only to that person—you capitalize it.

- Secretary of State
- Speaker of the House
- The President of the United

Rule Number Seven
When referring to animals, capitalize the part of the breed that is a proper noun or is derived from a proper noun; otherwise lowercase.

-

- German shepherd
- Irish wolfhound
- English bulldog
- boxer
- cocker spaniel
- Bengal tiger
- California condor

- Maine coon
- Kodiak bear
- Texas longhorn

Let's take a look at dog breeds specifically. "Great Dane," "Great Pyrenees," "Old English sheepdog," and "Bracco Italiano" are among a few of the exceptions. Every source I checked had them listed as "Great Dane," "Great Pyrenees," and "Bracco Italiano," all with initial caps, but I couldn't find a reason. The only reason I could think of is that the first names are considered part of the name, just like *general* in "General Patton" would be capitalized.

If you wanted to tell someone they had a great German shepherd, that would be okay, but it would look odd to say "great great Dane," because then we might think we're referring to the dog's ancestry and not saying that the dog is wonderful. If it were capitalized, though, as in "great Great Dane," it wouldn't look out of place.

Following the theory that the capitalization follows the way a dog is named, I'm guessing "Miniature Australian Shepherd" would also be capitalized, although I can't find a resource to back that up.

With all the other breeds I checked, the word that required capitalization occurred first: "Irish setter," "German shepherd," "Anatolian shepherd," etc.

One more exception goes against the rules the other way: *dalmatian* is often seen lowercased. Many dictionaries list it this way, though there is typically a note that it is often seen capitalized. But why it's not capitalized is beyond me because it derives its name from Dalmatia, a region of Croatia, so by all accounts it should be capitalized.

The only possible explanation is that some suggest the

origin of the breed was not Dalmatia but ancient Egypt or
another part of the Mediterranean Sea, which would seem to
negate the capitalization based on a geographic region.
However, I don't know if I agree. The rule says if a breed is
named *after* a region, you capitalize it. It doesn't say it had to
originate in the region.

There is a lot of contention regarding the capitalization of
dog breeds. Many, including most of those associated with the
American Kennel Club, do not follow the suggested guidelines. They capitalize all recognized breeds.

The results of two Google Ngram searches follow. One
shows "Great Dane," "great Dane," "German shepherd," and
"German Shepherd." The second shows "English sheepdog,"
"English Sheepdog," "Great Pyrenees," "great Pyrenees,"
"Yorkshire Terrier," and "Yorkshire terrier."

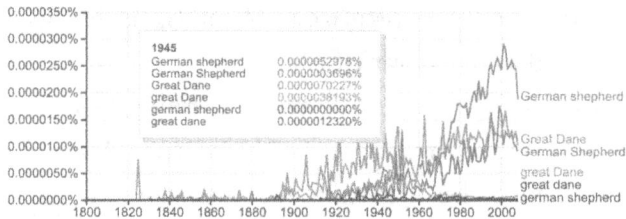

Great Dane, German shepherd

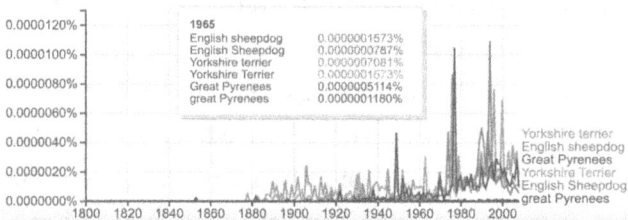

English sheepdog, Yorkshire terrier, Great Pyrenees

The Ngram searches reflect the style-guide rules for the

most part; however, when you analyze social media (Facebook posts and blogs), you'll see they paint a different picture, and the capitalization used is much closer to that supported by the AKC.

The capitalization of dog, cat, and horse breeds, etc., is so widespread I don't see it presenting a problem—as long as you're consistent.

For a more comprehensive look at the capitalization of animal breeds, see the animal breed section of this book.

Rule Number Eight

Capitalize food names only when they contain a proper noun.

- Italian dressing
- Louisiana hot sauce
- Kentucky Fried Chicken (now KFC)

In some cases, there are exceptions to this also. Examples follow, and they are all from the major dictionaries.

- Caesar salad
- Brussels sprouts
- Waldorf salad
- french fries
- Boston cream pie
- napoleon

A curious person might wonder why it isn't "French Fries." I looked this up in several dictionaries. Most had it lowercased, although a few had it capitalized as an option. I found one dictionary that had the capitalized version listed first and the lowercase as the option.

As far as *napoleon* goes, I didn't understand why it wasn't capitalized either.

I continued researching, determined to uncover the truth. After much work, I finally found an explanation and not only for *napoleon* but for "french fries."

Napoleon

I had always known what a napoleon was, but I associated it with the emperor Napoleon. Little did I realize the name came from my ancestral city of Naples.

The napoleon, for those of you who don't know, is a flaky pastry layered with custard and icing. The dessert's original name was napolitain, referring to its origin (the city of Naples, Italy). Below or on the next page is a picture of a napoleon.

I discovered the history of napoleons, but I still don't understand why they're not capitalized, even when they were named after Naples—that's a proper noun.

Now to address the issue with "french fries." It wasn't until I looked for information regarding the capitalization of *napoleons* that I discovered the following about "french fries."

There doesn't seem to be conclusive evidence, but what I found persuaded me enough that I included it.

One version states that "french fries" was a dish invented in Belgium that had been a popular food source for years.

During WWI, American soldiers were introduced to these "fried potatoes," and since the people spoke French, the Americans named the dish "french fries."

Another version is that they are so named because the potatoes are "frenched," not because they're a French invention. I hesitated when I read this because I was not familiar with the word *frenched*.

I looked it up in several dictionaries, finding it in *Merriam-Webster's*. Below is the definition:

---

french verb, often capitalized
\ 'french \
frenched; **frenching**; **frenches**
Definition of *french* *transitive verb*
: to trim the meat from the end of the bone of (something, such as a chop)
: to cut (green beans) in thin lengthwise strips before cooking

---

I not only got an answer about why these words weren't capitalized, I learned a lot as well.

Rule Number Nine

Capitalize the first word in a complete quotation, even if it occurs in mid-sentence.

- John Paul Jones is reputed to have said, "Give me liberty or give me death," just before dying.

Rule Number Ten
Capitalizing academic degrees and job titles
The Chicago Manual of Style (CMOS) recommends writing academic degrees in lower case except when directly preceding or following a name. Proper nouns, of course, should still be capitalized.
Examples:

- Carlos is pursuing a bachelor of science in civil engineering.
- Carlos is pursuing a bachelor of arts in English.
- He introduced Jennifer Miller, Master of Fine Arts.
- He introduced Master of Fine Arts Jennifer Miller.

There is agreement, however, that abbreviations of academic degrees are to be capitalized. CMOS recommends omitting periods unless required for tradition or consistency (BA, BS, MA, MS, PhD), but AP prefers the periods (B.A., B.S., M.A., M.S., Ph.D.).

An exception is that CMOS makes allowances for capitalizing the spelled-out version of degrees when listed on business cards or used on résumés (when cited as the degree achieved, not in running text).

Capitalize degrees on business cards, on diplomas, or when displayed in a directory or resume. Lowercase them in running text, where they are almost always generic in nature. Some contexts—especially in an academic publication or in advertising—suggest that a specific degree is being named, and it's common to capitalize: "All applicants for the Master's in Cerebral Cosmetic Surgery should send $24,000 in unmarked bills to the Bob's Your Uncle Online University at the address below." But even then, a master's in cerebral cosmetic surgery is generic in that anyone with the cash can have one, so lowercasing it (per Chicago style) would also be fine.

— CMOS

Rule Number Eleven

Titles of works

There are several ways to approach this topic, and there are numerous rules associated with it. The most sensible approach seems to suffice for almost all situations. The following list consists of words not to capitalize in titles of books, songs, movies, and other works of art:

- *a, an, and, at, but, by, for, in, nor, of, on, or, out, so, the, to, up,* and *yet.*

All other words, you capitalize (as well as *any* word (even if in the above list) that is the first or last words in the title).

- Capitalize the title's first and last word.
- Capitalize all adjectives, adverbs, and nouns.
- Capitalize all pronouns (including *it*).
- Capitalize all verbs, including the verb *to be* in all forms (*is*, *are*, *was*, *has been*, etc.).
- Capitalize *no*, *not*, and the interjection *O* (e.g., *How Long Must I Wait, O Lord?*).
- Do not capitalize an article (*a*, *an*, *the*) unless it is first or last word in the title.

The following title would be capitalized like this.
☑ The Time for Peace Is Up.
✖ the Time for Peace is up.
☑ Of Mice and Men
✖ of Mice and Men

- Do not capitalize a **coordinating conjunction** (a connecting word), such as
  and, *or*, *no*r, *but*, *for*, *yet*, *so*, unless it is first or last in the title.
- Do not capitalize the word *to*, with or without an infinitive, unless it is first or last in the title.

There are other rules governing how to cite works of art. Some should be in italics, some enclosed with quotation marks, and some underlined. For a comprehensive discussion of the rules, I suggest you refer to the style guide you use because they may differ.

Rule Number Twelve

Capitalization with geographical terms (compass points)

There are a lot of rules related to capitalizing geographical terms, but the ones mentioned below should suffice for most issues. We'll cover it in more detail later.

If you're using *north*, *south*, *east*, *northeast*, etc., to indicate a direction, lowercase; however, if you're using these words to indicate a specific region, capitalize them. Examples follow:

- I gave my sister directions to come visit me: go south for about six hundred miles, and when you see a sign that says "Welcome to the South," turn right.
- To reach the beach, drive south for an hour, then go east for two hours.
- He lives on the Eastern Shore (a specific spot in MD).
- She moved to the West Coast, not the Ivory Coast.
- He was born in the Mid Atlantic, but he moved to the Midwest about two years ago.
- It was easy to tell who was speaking; he has a noticeable Southern accent.

Rule Number Thirteen
Heavenly Bodies
Earth is lowercase except when used as a proper noun.

☑ The third planet from the sun is the *Earth*.

☑ He loves the cool, moist feeling of digging through *earth* when he plants things.

☑ *Earth* is one of eight planets in our solar system. (They used to say there were nine.)

✕ He's a down-to-Earth person.

✕ Mary? She's the salt of the Earth.

Rule Number Fourteen
Capitalization when dealing with race/ethnicities

Capitalize the names of races, nationalities, tribes, etc.: Italian, German, Caucasian, Japanese, Chinese, Middle Eastern, Oriental, but you would use lowercase with terms like *black* or *white*.

Rule Number Fifteen
Company names

Capitalize company names the same way you would individual names. Also abbreviate and capitalize *corporation (corp.), incorporated (inc.), limited (ltd.)*, etc., when those words are used following the name.

- 3M Company
- Abbott Laboratories
- American Express Company
- AT&T Corp.
- Bank of America Corporation

You keep the capitalization even if you don't use *Co., Corp., Inc., Ltd.*, etc., when following the names.

- Apple Inc.
- Apple
- General Motors Company
- General Motors
- Samsung Electronics Co., Ltd.
- Samsung

Rule Number Sixteen
Capitalization of brand names

Capitalize company names as well as recognized brand names: Apple, Google, Coca Cola, Cadillac, etc., but also the following.

- Band-Aid
- Bubble Wrap
- Chapstick
- Crock-Pot
- eBay
- Frisbee
- iPhone
- iPad
- Jacuzzi
- Jeep
- Kevlar
- Kleenex
- Kool-Aid
- Memory Stick
- Onesies
- Popsicle
- Post-it
- Q-tip
- Rollerblade
- Scotch Tape
- Sharpie
- Styrofoam
- Teflon
- Tupperware

Note how three of the product names have a lowercase initial letter: iPhone, iPad, and eBay. That's because the companies want the words formatted that way. It's part of their branding.

There are many more brand names that require capitalization, but these are some of the more common ones. If you suspect an item is a brand name, check with your dictionary or do an online search before committing to a course of action.

Rule Number Seventeen
Capitalization with roads
Capitalize the names of specific roads, highways, turn-pikes, etc.

- U.S. Route 66
- Interstate 95
- Pennsylvania Turnpike
- Baltimore Parkway

But lowercase the following:

- I take the turnpike from Philadelphia to Pittsburgh.
- Is there an interstate that goes to Atlanta?
- I need to drive to California, but I'd like to go via U.S. highways, not interstates.

Rule Number Eighteen
(Government organizations and political parties)
Government organizations, political parties, names of specific courts, etc., are all capitalized.

- Grand Old Party (GOP)
- The Supreme Court
- Yellowstone National Park
- Big Bend National Park
- Federal Bureau of Investigation
- Central Intelligence Agency

Political Parties

You capitalize political organizations, such as the Republican Party, the Democratic Party, the Libertarian, etc. But you don't capitalize the words when used in the common sense.

- He's a lifelong democrat.
- She always votes republican.
- For the first time they both voted democratic.
- She's a long-time member of the Republican Party.
- He campaigns relentlessly for the Democratic Party.

If used jointly or in the plural sense, though, the word *party* or *parties* would not be capitalized because it would no longer be a part of the name as it would not be connected. It is much like the reasoning behind why a word may lose its capitalization when a comma or other words come between it and the named party. Let's look at a few examples.

- The presidential candidates all come from the Democratic or Republican parties.
- The Budget and Finance committees.

AP Stylebook suggests lowercasing any title that is separated from a person's name.

- When Obama was president, there were kids in the White House for the first time in years.
- As the former chairman of Apple, Steve Jobs wielded his power mercilessly.

Rule Number Nineteen
Names of Organizations or Institutions

- American Diabetes Association
- American Medical Association
- American Cancer Society
- The Mystery Writers Guild

But you'd say, "He's a member of a medical association or "She donates to various cancer societies."

Rule Number Twenty
Awards and Medals
Capitalize named awards, medals, military decorations, etc.

- Heisman Trophy
- Academy Award
- Golden Globe
- Medal of Honor
- Purple Heart
- Pulitzer Prize

Rule Number Twenty-One
Rooms, Suites, Offices
Capitalize *room* only when it is part of the name. The following is from *Chicago*.

Official names of rooms, offices, and the like are capitalized.

The Empire Room (*but* room 421)

The Amelia Earhart Suite (*but* suite 219)

The Lincoln Bedroom
The Oval Office
The West Wing of the White House

— CMOS

- The wedding was held in the Green Room.
- The reception will be held in the Bridal Room.
- The White House has had many famous guests stay in the Lincoln Room.
- Governor Adams is in room 477.
- Room 1212 is reserved for Ms. Marsano.

But if referring to multiple rooms, it isn't capitalized (when *rooms* follows the proper nouns):

- The ceremonies were held in the Green and Gold rooms.

- Remember to reserve rooms #412, #615, and #1410 for the senators, as per their request.

Also to note, if a letter is joined to the room number, it isn't hyphenated.

- Room A17 is available.
- He always requests room 1010B.

Part One

NAMES, TITLES OF PEOPLE, JOB TITLES

You'd think the capitalization of names and titles would be easy, but it represents one of the more challenging aspects of capitalization.

This confusion is not restricted to nonprofessionals. Writers are often forced to resort to the dictionary to verify a spelling, and while there's nothing wrong with that, the word they're looking for is often not listed.

Because of this, it's best to learn the rules that govern and guide capitalization for all things.

NAMES AND TITLES OF PEOPLE

Capitalize a person's name as well as their title and any suffixes:

- George W. Bush was not technically a *junior*.
- Bob Walker *Jr.* was named after his father. He plans to name his son Bob Walker *III*.
- *Mrs.* Sebastian has been a widow for years.
- *President* Obama was the first black *president*.
- *Vice President* Biden may run for office in 2020.
- Abraham Lincoln was *president* during one of the country's more trying times.

Job titles should only be capitalized when they are part of the person's name (usually preceding it). We'll cover this in more detail in the section on job titles.

Titles are usually capitalized when they precede a name, but only if there are no interrupting words. If a word or comma comes between the title and name, it is (not capitalized)

- My doctor, Paul Cunningham, is a nice guy (no caps due to comma).
- Dr. Paul Cunningham is a nice guy.
- The president, Barack Obama, is a personable guy (no caps due to comma).
- President Obama is a personable guy.

We've already discussed job titles that follow a person's name (not capitalized), but let's look at job titles used in place of a person's name. I'm not speaking of using the title when directly addressing the person, as in "Good morning, Captain." The examples that follow show what I mean.

- The director of marketing will visit Atlanta on Thursday.
- Jenny Shellport, the director of marketing, will visit Atlanta on Thursday.
- Director of Marketing Jenny Shellport will visit Atlanta on Thursday.

Looking at the above, you can see that in the first example, we refer to *the director of marketing* in place of her name (Jenny Shellport) but we didn't address her directly, therefore, it doesn't get capitalized.

It doesn't matter what the job title is. A high-ranking office is treated the same as any other.

- The *governor* called a budget meeting.
- The *mayor* frequently walks the city.

- The *president* will be in the city this week.

Now that I've said that, we need to visit the exceptions, the ones you knew would be there.

If you use a person's title in a direct address (as we showed above with *Captain*), the title needs to be capitalized.

- I need to see you, Lieutenant.
- Mom, can I go out tonight?
- I think we should talk, Pastor.

But if it's not a direct address, the titles are lowercased.

- I need to see the lieutenant.
- I asked my mom if I could go out tonight.
- I think I should talk to the pastor.

This will be covered in more detail in the chapter regarding capitalization and dialogue.

The other rule is for when the title replaces the name of a few of the highest-ranking (usually a one-of-a-kind) people:

- The President of the United States.
- The Queen of England.
- The Speaker of the House.
- The Secretary of State.

If you speaking about the person holding that office currently, you could capitalize the title since there is only one of them.

- The Speaker of the House will address Congress tonight.
- The Secretary of State meets with the Iranian ambassador tomorrow.
- The President is expected to veto the bill at today's meeting.
- The Queen is hosting a dinner party for all diplomats.

This is a choice to be made by the writer, and as long as there is consistency, either way should be fine.

Following Signatures

Titles may be capitalized even when following a name when it is used with a signature on a formal letter.

Sincerely,

Jane Doe, Vice President of Human Resources

Nicknames

Nicknames should be capitalized when used in place of real names.

- Joey *"Four Eyes"* is the one you're lookin' for.
- *Doggs* never had a light for his smokes.
- *Slick* has been on his way to prison for seventeen years.

You *do not* capitalize terms of endearment like *honey* or *sugar*.

Do not capitalize a person's job descriptor or occupation.

- It wouldn't be *Police Officer* John Smith.
- It would be *police officer* John Smith.

"Police officer" is his *job* not his title. He may be a sergeant or a patrolman, but "police officer" is the job he performs. It's no different than if you had a job as a carpenter. You wouldn't be referred to as Carpenter John Smith.

If *carpenter* became part of a title, then it would be capitalized. An example would be if you achieved a higher level of craftsmanship, you might be called "Master Carpenter John Smith."

Chapter Two

JOB TITLES

I've duplicated a couple of listings in this chapter. I hope you don't mind, but I felt it was worthwhile to go over them again as they are so often misused.

I've mentioned before how crazy the business world is regarding capitalization. I sometimes think many people over-capitalize because they feel that capitalizing a word makes it seem more important, which means that, by association, *they* are more important. The truth is they will likely become more important by getting it right. Now, let's look at a few of the more common errors and how to write them correctly.

Many of these we have already dealt with in the section on names and titles, but that section dealt with titles of all types, and this section is restricted to business use.

Likewise, it doesn't matter how high up the corporate ladder one climbs, the rules apply to all.

☑ Bill DeMarco was just named chairman of the board.

✖ Bill DeMarco was just named Chairman of the Board.

✘ The company's new President, Hector Ruiz, starts Monday.

☑ The company's new president, Hector Ruiz, starts Monday.

☑ On Monday, President Hector Ruiz starts work.

✘ Hector Ruiz, the new President, starts on Monday.

When a title is used generically to describe your position or complement your job description, keep it lowercased. Below are a few instances when you would and would not capitalize your title.

On a résumé, if you're listing the title as the position you held at a company during a specific time period, you'd capitalize it.

- XYZ Company, 5/2001–5/2019 *Director of Quality*

In a cover letter, when writing about your experience, you'd keep it lowercased.

Dear Mark:

- I served as *director of quality* for eighteen years at XYZ Company.

Imagine a scenario where you interviewed for this job and got it. A few days later, you receive the offer letter.

Dear Josh:

- We are pleased to offer you the position of *vice president of quality assurance* at PDQ Corporation. Your starting salary will be . . .

Perhaps you're offended by them not capitalizing your

new title, but why should they? If they had sent that offer to a bricklayer, would that title be capitalized? Let's take a look.

- We are pleased to offer you the position of *bricklayer* at Ferraro Construction. Your starting salary will be . . .

*A*nd capitalization rules don't stop at corporate America's doorstep. Look at a few of the following.

- The school principal made an announcement after the incident. If any student has a problem dealing with this, please consult your guidance counselor (not *Guidance Counselor*).
- Professor Shelly Burnham retired. A new professor will take her place in a few weeks, but in the interim, an *assistant professor* of Spanish will step in.
- Any further incidents will be dealt with harshly by Vice Principal Frank Marsh. And remember, he didn't get to be vice principal by being nice.

Named divisions and departments within a company are usually capitalized.

- He is a sales manager.
- He is the sales manager for the *Eastern Division*.
- She heads up finance for the *Portable Device Division* (PDD).

If a division of a company or a department within that company are specifically named, capitalize it.

- The *Advertising Department* sent a memo for all to see. (*named* dept)
- Joan recently joined an *advertising department* in retail.

You capitalize it if it refers to a specific department even if *department* is not mentioned.

- Bruce is the new vice president of *Advertising* (meaning the department, not the function).

Statements like the one above can be tricky. If used to mean Bruce is the new vice president of advertising as a function—meaning he's in charge of advertising—keep it lowercased. In that sense, advertising may be a function of marketing. But if you mean to say he was in charge of the department titled Advertising, it should be capitalized.

When using the words *committee*, *department*, *division*, *group*, etc., as part of a recognized name, those words should be capitalized. But if those words are used generically, they remain lowercased.

- The *Health Committee* (name of the committee), established by the *Human Resources Department*, evaluated the new insurance plan.
- The committee evaluated the new health insurance plan.
- The committee established by the *Human Resources Department* evaluated the new insurance plan.

Whether it involves a cover letter, job description, résumé, or any other writing, job skills are generally not capitalized (unless they contain formal names or proper nouns).

✖ I have seven years' experience Programming and developing Inventory Control Systems for the Biotechnology Industry.

✔ I have seven years' experience programming and developing inventory control systems for the biotechnology industry.

That example brought up another over-capitalized usage —industries. Industries are no different than anything else, and none of them are more significant simply because you work in them. The following should all be lowercase.

- pharmaceutical industry
- biotechnology industry
- medical device industry
- automobile industry
- food and hospitality industry
- retail goods industry
- shipping industry
- entertainment industry

And while that is a small sample of the number of industries, the rest follow suit.

- He's a vice president of regulatory affairs in the medical device industry.
- She just took a job as director of marketing in the telecommunications industry.
- His father was a bigwig in the pharmaceutical industry, so he got in easy.

Let's review the department, division, group designation again.

☑ Ken works in finance.

Finance is lowercase here because he could be working in finance anywhere. He could be a financial analyst with ABC Company, or he could be an accounting manager with XYZ Company.

☑ Ken works in the Finance Department (presuming that is the name of the department).

If the name of the department is Financial Control, it would be "Ken works in the finance department," meaning the department that handles finance. And assuming that is correct, it would be "Ken works in Financial Control."

When the term refers to a function or area of expertise, do not capitalize it.

- Bob is a financial expert. He is considered a finance wiz.
- She is the best marketing manager I know.
- Have some marketing people review this sales plan.
- Have some people from the Marketing Department review this sales plan.

The bottom line: you capitalize the name of the department only when you know it is the name of the department. What you may refer to as the "Sales Department" may actually be the Marketing and Sales Department. Or asking to speak to the Purchasing Department may, in fact, be erroneous because purchasing may simply be a group within the Materials Management Department.

The way to deal with division or any of the other words is the same. If you say you work for the Personal Computer

Division, it needs to be named that, not simply that you work for a division of the company that makes personal computers. If it's not named Personal Computer Division, that's not where you say you work (or at least you don't capitalize it).

To sum up what we've covered, let's look at a few more examples:

- The manager of quality is Jane Miller.
- Jane Miller is a quality manger at XYZ Company.
- Jane Miller, manager of quality for XYZ Company, will be visiting on Tuesday.
- I don't know if it will happen, but the president may accompany her, not the country's president, but the president of XYZ.

In some cases, writers may choose to capitalize *president* in one or both cases, but if they do, they'll be going against the recommendations of both style guides (CMOS and AP).

When dealing with organizations that have their own style guides, they may elect to capitalize the upper management (usually VP and up). This is sometimes referred to as the ego rule.

If you write for a company that has such a recommendation in its style guide, you need to abide by it (at least if you want to continue writing for them).

Let's go over job titles one more time because it is an area that gives people a lot of trouble. And don't forget, job titles cross industries and occupations, so a job title in the pharmaceutical industry is no different than one in the automotive industry or a title for a government employee.

Imagine seeing the following positions advertised in your local paper. Which ones have correct capitalization?

- The position for Chief Financial Officer for XYZ
  Corporation is accepting submissions as of June 30.
- William Smythson, President of Disk Drives of
  America, will be interviewing candidates personally
  at the San Diego job fair.
- Chef's Unlimited will be accepting submissions
  from serious candidates only (i.e., ones with PhD's
  in Culinary Arts) beginning on Friday, July 7.
- Anand Kunrathy, Dean of the School of Medicine,
  will be the final decision maker regarding who gets
  hired as the Chief Medical Officer.

Although it's unlikely you'll ever see positions advertised
with the capitalization that is recommended, the fact is, none
of the above positions should have been capitalized. They
should have looked like the following:

- The position for chief financial officer for XYZ
  Corporation is accepting submissions as of June 30.
- William Smythson, president of Disk Drives of
  America, will be interviewing candidates personally
  at the San Diego job fair.
- Chef's Unlimited will be accepting submissions
  from serious candidates only (i.e., ones with PhD's
  in culinary arts) beginning on Friday, July 7.
- Anand Kunrathy, dean of the School of Medicine,
  will be the final decision maker regarding who gets
  hired as the chief medical officer.

Even when dealing with the capitalization-happy government, guidelines should be followed. The following are all
correct—or are they?

- Lieutenant Johnson addressed the graduating class at the Naval Academy.
- Lt. Jeff Johnson gave a fine speech to the 110 graduates.
- U.S. Navy Lieutenant Jeff Johnson had been a graduate himself, twelve years earlier.
- Jeff Johnson, a recent Lieutenant, served five years of active duty.
- After Lieutenant Johnson finished, Admiral Gladstone addressed the eager graduates.

Now let's analyze the sentences to see which words *should* have been capitalized and which *shouldn't* have been.

☑ Lieutenant Johnson addressed the graduating class at the Naval Academy.

☑ Lt. Jeff Johnson gave a fine speech to the 110 graduates. (*Lt.* is abbreviated because his full name is used.)

✗ U.S. Navy Lieutenant Jeff Johnson had been a graduate himself, twelve years earlier. (*lieutenant* should be lowercase as "U.S. Navy Lieutenant" is not an actual title.)

✗ Jeff Johnson, a recent Lieutenant, served five years of active duty. (*lieutenant* should be lowercase as it comes after the name, and words separate it from his name)

☑ After Lieutenant Johnson finished, Admiral Gladstone addressed the eager graduates.

Chapter Three

GOVERNMENT POSITIONS, BUILDINGS, ORGANIZATIONS

*T*he government is no different than anything else when it comes to capitalization; at least according to CMOS and AP.

Named buildings or departments are treated as proper nouns, but if part of the name consists of a common noun, and that noun is used generically, it should be lowercased. Some examples may help explain:

- "Pennsylvania State Legislature" is capitalized.

used, keep the capitalization, as in "The State Legislature is meeting tonight" or even "The Legislature met last week."

But when speaking in general terms, no capital is required, as in "No state's legislature passed the bill."

The members of Congress are referred to as "senator" or "congressional member" when not affixed to a person's name or being addressed but capitalized otherwise:

- I just got to Washington, and I met three senators and two congressmen already.
- I just got to Washington, and I met Senator Richards, Senator McKeeves, and Congressman Marks.

The words *Army*, *Navy*, *Air Force*, *Marine Corps*, and *Coast Guard* are capitalized when referring to the United States armed forces, but not if they aren't preceded by the letters *U.S.* Here's *Chicago's* take on it:

Titles of armies, navies, air forces, fleets, regiments, battalions, companies, corps, and so forth are capitalized. Unofficial but well-known names, such as Green Berets, are also capitalized. Words such as *army* and *navy* are lowercased when standing alone, when used collectively in the plural, or when not part of an official title.

— CMOS

AP has a different stance. It suggests capitalizing *army, navy,* etc., even when standing alone—if referring to the U.S. branches but not foreign powers.

- U.S. Army
- U.S. Navy
- U.S. Marines
- U.S. Air Force

But when used generically, it is as follows:

- Brazil's army is substantial.
- Spain's navy (at one time) was a force to be reckoned with.
- He is a Marine.
- She became an airman when she graduated.

If you note, *Marine* is capitalized while the others are not. It isn't because Marines are any more special than the others; it's how the name derives. Members of the U.S. Army are called *soldiers,* of the Navy; *sailors,* and of the Air Force; *airmen,* but members of the U.S. Marines are known as *Marines,* hence the capitalization. (The same applies to Coastguardsmen.)

Chicago and AP differ on their treatment of this. *Chicago* recommends *marine* and AP recommends *Marine* when they are used alone. Both would recommend U.S. Marine.

On the following page should be an image of a fake organizational chart showing the relationship between members of Congress and members of the armed forces. Note the capitalization of each.

U.S. government

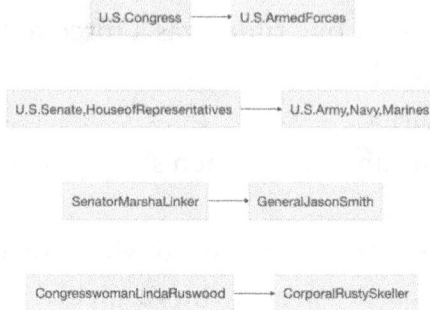

U.S.Congress ⟶ U.S.ArmedForces

U.S.Senate,HouseofRepresentatives ⟶ U.S.Army,Navy,Marines

SenatorMarshaLinker ⟶ GeneralJasonSmith

CongresswomanLindaRuswood ⟶ CorporalRustySkeller

But

MarshaLinker,senator ⟶ JasonSmith,five-stargeneral

While we're talking about the government, words such as *city*, *state*, *federal*, *naval*, and *national*, when used to modify or describe another word, are (not capitalized) The examples that follow are from a style guide used by the Naval Postgraduate School.

"There are federal regulations about the relationship of city and state governments"; "The city of New York is in the state of New York"; and "The new naval program begins tomorrow."

— NPS (NAVAL POSTGRADUATE SCHOOL)

Regarding other capitalization:

In "U.S. Congress," you would capitalize *Congress* even without the *U.S.* if it was clear you were referring to that single entity; however, if used in the adjectival form of *congressional* or if referring to any congress of people, you'd keep it lowercased.

"U.S. government" and the "federal government" are lowercased (except *U.S.*) because *government* is not a name, it is "the organization that is the governing authority," the body that governs.

As the previous chart shows, you treat members of the armed forces just like you would employees of a company. Governmental organizations and divisions are treated the same way.

If a division of the government is named, that specific name is capitalized, such as the "Internal Revenue Service" and the "Central Intelligence Agency." And those capitalization guidelines flow down the line, so within the "U.S. Armed Forces," it's "Army Rangers" (a named unit, similar to a department of a company) and "Green Berets."

"Navy SEAL" is capitalized for an extra reason: SEAL is capitalized because it is an acronym derived from "sea, air, and land."

"Special Forces" is also capitalized when referring specifically to that unit, as in "He trained for years, then joined the Special Forces," but it's not capitalized if used generically, as in "He was a special-forces type guy."

Numbered squadrons, battalions, regiments, etc., are capitalized:

- He led the 2nd Squadron.
- She joined the 4th Brigade

- The 7th Regiment was decimated.
- Reinforcements are coming! The 21st Infantry Division is on its way.

A reminder: There is disagreement among style guides regarding the capitalization of military branches when mentioned alone, that is, without *U.S.* preceding the word. CMOS says not to, but AP says yes.

I think—like other things—if it's obvious (from context or previous referrals) you're referring to a specific branch of the military, capitalize it. If there is a question, don't.

Part Two

GEOGRAPHIC LOCATIONS, TOPOGRAPHICAL POINTS, AND POLITICAL DIVISIONS

If job titles and deciding when to capitalize them presents a problem, when to capitalize geographical locations dwarfs that issue. Primary topographical points don't seem to be a problem, at least not the ones most are familiar with, such as the Statue of Liberty or the Washington Monument.

However, geographical locations and when to capitalize compass points like southern, northern, eastern, western, and such are the main culprits.

Knowing whether to write "south Philadelphia" or "South Philadelphia" follows the same logic as determining whether to write "northern Alabama" or "Northern Alabama."

Chapter Four

GEOGRAPHIC LOCATIONS AND COMPASS POINTS

*I*ncluded in this section are topographical locations, specific regional locations, and compass points. First let's look at the rules.

- If a term identifies a specific (unique) area (continents, countries, states or provinces, regions, cities, districts, etc.), then it is capitalized.

The same would apply to words that derive from that specific word. An example would be "Anatolian shepherd" because it is derived from Anatolia, a region in Turkey. Another example would be "Texas longhorn," which is derived from the name of the state where the breed originated.

- If a term is unique to a regional or local area, capitalize it.

Once again, examples follow. In many major cities, you

will find specifically named areas: Little Italy, Chinatown, or possibly the Riverfront.

New York City has SoHo (south of Houston), and Maryland has its Eastern Shore. Both areas are recognizable by anyone who lives or has lived there.

On a more global scale, we have the Sunbelt or the West Coast, in the United States, and the Ivory Coast of Africa, and even areas made famous for other reasons: the Bermuda Triangle and the Silicon Valley.

- Capitalize compass points when they refer to a specific geographical region or when they are part of a place-name or street name. If used for direction only, or if they refer to a region in general, keep them lowercased.

Examples of both are below:

- the Northeast
- the western Hemisphere*
- Northern Europe
- Southern Italy
- Central America
- Eastern Europe
- the Midwest
- East End
- North End
- the South
- the North Atlantic
- South Pacific
- Southeast Asia

* "Western Hemisphere" was lowercased in most dictionaries I checked with, but a few had it capitalized.

A few names are always referred to with *the* preceding it, but in most cases, *the* is (not capitalized) A few examples are shown below:

- the Atlantic
- the South
- the Northern Hemisphere
- the North Pole
- the South of France

As far as referring to a region in general, the following would be lowercased.

- southern Maine
- western Idaho
- eastern Virginia

But when the region is typically referred to using the compass point and is known as a specific region, capitalize it.

- Southern California
- South Side of Chicago (or Chicago's South Side)
- West Philadelphia
- West Texas

If the region mentioned is a known political division, such as North Korea or South Vietnam, capitalize it.

If you have questions (or if the dictionary doesn't list it), I would suggest keeping it lowercased.

When any compass point designates a specific region or is a part of a proper noun, capitalize it.

- His family lives in the North.
- His new job took him to the Deep South.
- Being from New York, he was pleasantly surprised by Southern hospitality.
- What she dreamed of was finding a job on the Eastern Shore (Maryland's Eastern Shore).

Any use of the words to provide directions, are always lowercased.

- To get where you want to go, head *west* for six miles, then go *north* for ten.
- California? It's about three thousand miles due *west*.
- Florida is a large state when you consider the *north-to-south* distance.

Words like *southern, northern, western, and eastern* are often used to describe cultural or political types. If they are used in that manner, capitalize them.

- Florida gets crowded in the winter, especially with the influx of *Northeasterners*.
- *Southerners* like to relax during hot, summer days.
- The *Northeast* is generally considered to include New England as well as New York, Pennsylvania, and New Jersey.
- *Southern* hospitality is a well-established tradition in the *Southern* states.

- When Silicon Valley first started, *Eastern* bankers stood out because of their style of dress.

If the compass points refer to climate though, keep it lowercased.

- Alabama's *southern* temperatures push the heat index into triple figures quite often.
- The *northern* winds and snowstorms keep Wyoming uncomfortably cold for five or six months.
- The *western* winds of California make the forests susceptible to wildfires.

Remember, if the compass point is used when referring to a *specific* area, capitalize it, but if it is used to refer to a region in general, lowercase it.

- My son lives in the *Northeast*.
- His ex-wife moved to one of the *southeastern* states.
- The *Southwest* tends to be hot and dry.
- The *western* part of the country gets far less rain than the *eastern* half.

If a compass point term is used to define a company's sales district or organizational structure, capitalize it.

- He took a new job as manager of the *Southern* District.
- The *Northern* Territory was the most lucrative as it included New York, Boston, and Philadelphia.
- The *Western* Region's sales were up almost twenty

percent, thanks to increases from San Francisco and Los Angeles.

Sometimes a region is defined in the minds of the region's inhabitants, but specific geographic boundaries remain unclear. Such is the case with the term "West Texas."

"West Texas" has no specific marker that designates a dividing line. It is thought of almost in terms of climate, and it indicates the separation of the wet, rainy climate of East Texas from the arid lands of West Texas.

A lot of people might say the dividing line runs from Del Rio in the south, through Abilene, to Wichita Falls. If you ask five more people, though, you're likely to get at least three different answers.

Regardless, in each person's eyes, the region itself is distinct from the rest of the state.

Other regions are more defined. Southern California is generally considered to encompass the eight southernmost counties, although a few consider it to extend as far north as San Luis Obispo. Despite that, many sources keep it lowercased.

Southern California

The Eastern Shore is very defined. It refers to the part of Maryland that lies east of the Chesapeake Bay.

The Texas Panhandle (often known as just the "Panhandle") is a rectangular piece of the northwest part of the state bordered by Oklahoma and New Mexico.

When terms are used for general location, they are (not capitalized)

- My brother lives in *northern* New Jersey.
- My sister lives in *southern* Pennsylvania.

Sometimes the local inhabitants of an area feel strongly about identifying with that region, and as a result, may elect to capitalize it. As long as they're consistent, I don't see a problem. An example might be Eastern Kentucky. A lot of people outside Kentucky may not think it should be capitalized, but it defines a specific region made up of thirty counties and encompassing the Eastern Kentucky coalfields.

Another thing to note is referring to a region with a capital letter when there is an existing locale close by. A few examples follow:

If you reference "south San Francisco" and you mean the southern part of San Francisco, keep it lowercased as there is a separate city named "South San Francisco" just to the south.

The same applies for "east St. Louis" and "East St. Louis."

You also need to be careful because a section of the location you're speaking about might be named the same, as is the case with "South Chicago."

If you say the South Side of Chicago, you are referring to a specific part of the city. Chicago's South Side neighborhood is bordered by East 79th Street on the north, South Chicago Avenue on the south and southwest, and the Calumet River on the southeast.

If you don't mean to refer to that specific region, do not use a capital letter for *south*, although it may be wiser to reword the sentence.

Another one to consider is San Francisco's famous "North Beach" section. Anyone who lives there is bound to know it, as are many others, but certainly not everyone, so you need to make sure you capitalize it properly.

As a final note, you almost never capitalize the compass point if it precedes the words "part of," "region of," or "section of," etc. The only exception I know of is "the South of France."

But again, it would only be capitalized when referred to as a specific region, not as a general area:

☑ My friend lives in the South of France.

☑ The best vineyards are in the South of France.

✗ The Pyrenees Mountains lie to the south of France.

✗ Spain and Portugal lie south of France.

Example three may be confusing at first because of the use of the article *the*: however, if you examine it closely, it is referring to a general geographic location south of France. It is not referring to the specific region known as "the South of France." It would have been better to reword it: "The Pyrenees Mountains lie south of France."

- His family was from the southern *part of* California.
- She visited the southern *part of* Italy and loved it.
- The northern *section of* Canada is extremely cold.
- The Pyrenees Mountains lie in the northern *region of* Spain.

If you encounter a situation where you're not sure whether to capitalize the word, and presuming the word isn't listed in the dictionary, consider rewriting the sentence to something like the above, then you'll know to keep it lowercased. I'll provide an example.

Instead of . . .

- She visited Southern Italy and loved it.

You may be uncertain about the capitalization of *southern*, so reword the sentence.

- She visited the southern part of Italy and loved it.

Now you know how to capitalize it because you used "part of," and when you do that, it's always lowercased.

You had no reason to worry because "Southern Italy" has long been recognized as a distinct region, but it's always better to be safe than sorry.

This is a common dilemma because many tend to capitalize regions whether they should be or not. Another example is "Southern California." I capitalized it earlier because it is a designated region, but many sources suggest lowercase. If you want to avoid a potential mistake, do as we suggest for "Southern Italy" and write, "southern part of California."

On the other hand, specific regions preceded by *Little* almost always need capitalization:

- Little Egypt
- Little Russia
- Little Italy
- Little Poland

The reason for the above is because when *little* is used in this fashion, it is referring to a very specific region (usually where a particular ethnic group settled), which restricts it to a defined region.

MORE ON CAPITALIZING GEOGRAPHIC REGIONS

As mentioned previously, capitalization of geographic terms is a major problem. There are generalized rules, but nothing even close to specific.

It would take a monumental effort to attempt to list all the geographical points that should be capitalized because it would include any specific region that has been given a name including a compass point.

Considering this, designated parts of states, regions, countries, continents, cities, neighborhoods, parks, etc., would all be capitalized. Look at the following (and this is just from Philadelphia).

- West Philadelphia
- South Philadelphia.
- Center City
- Little Italy
- Jeweler's Row

- Chinatown
- Rittenhouse Square

If you tried to list the New York sites, you'd have a much larger list.

We've already discussed how many geographic terms aren't listed as entries in dictionaries. But there is still a good way to tell if a place name should be capitalized.

Rule For Capitalizing Place Names

If the name indicates a specific place and no other, it should be capitalized. If someone says "Let's go to South Philly," and you know exactly what (and where) they're talking about, it should be capitalized. For instance, there is a place in Texas called the Hill Country.

If you ask anyone who's lived in Texas for even a short while, they will likely know where you mean. They may not know the exact coordinates, but they'd know it's a region west and northwest of San Antonio and southwest of Austin.

But you may not know that if you don't live in Texas, so how do you find out? Wikipedia is a great resource for this (and almost all geographic place-name questions). While some people have complained about the few inaccuracies found in Wikipedia, overall they've been pretty good. And they're sure as hell a lot better than a guess.

If Wikipedia has the place-name you're looking for, and if they list it as a specific point, not just a generalized area, it deserves a capital.

I looked up *Texas Hill Country*, and the below screenshot was listed as the area comprising the Hill Country, which goes to show it is definitely specific.

Notice I capitalized "Hill Country" above. I did so because I was referring to that specific region of Texas, not just any hilly country.

Another region I checked was Southern Italy. I'd seen several grammar sites and other blogs list it as "southern Italy."

It puzzled me because I've been to Italy, and if there's anything that's true, it's that the people recognize a distinct difference between Southern and Northern Italy.

To verify this, I checked Wikipedia again, and the screen-shot below is what I found. This is the same screenshot I used earlier.

Not only it *Southern Italy* considered a distinct region, the Italian people have a name they refer to it as: *mezzogiorno,* which means "midday," and as the map shows, it is made up of specific regions.

You'll find the same with other places you look up.

- South Philadelphia
- Chicago's South Side
- Boston's North End
- New York's Upper East Side

*T*here are a few individual words that may present what appears to be a problem at first. Words such as *mecca* or *utopia* are capitalized—or not—depending on use. If you are referring to Mecca, as in the Islamic city, it is capitalized. And if you are referring to Utopia (the imaginary place in Thomas More's satirical work), that is also capitalized. But if either of those words is used generically, as in "I love the lake. It is a utopia" or "The cabin at the lake is a mecca for stressed-out people," the words are (not capitalized)

Summary

The bottom line is that if you have a question regarding the capitalization of a geographic region and you need to know if it is a specifically defined region, check it out in Wikipedia. If you feel more comfortable, use Google or another search engine to verify it.

By the way, we mentioned Eastern Kentucky previously. While further checking, I discovered there is a city named Eastern in Kentucky, so you would need to be specific when referring to it. The city would be Eastern, Kentucky (formatted with a comma after *Eastern*), and the region would be Eastern Kentucky (no comma).

You'll be safe following these instructions, and if the company or person you're writing for follows a style guide that disagrees with anything I've said, the safe bet is to rewrite using "part of" so you can keep the term lowercased.

If you still can't decide, the safer choice is to keep the word lowercased.

As a note: I had *hemisphere* and all geographic designations of it (*eastern, northern* etc.) as lowercased originally because the dictionaries I looked them up in spelled the words that way, but since then I've looked elsewhere. Here's what I found:

Eastern Hemisphere:

- American Heritage.
- Dictionary.com.
- AP Stylebook.
- Webster's New World College Dictionary

All of the above capitalized *Western, Eastern, Northern,* and *Southern Hemisphere.* The rest of the dictionaries I checked with didn't.

Chapter Five

TOPOGRAPHICAL POINTS, STREETS, AND MAN-MADE STRUCTURES

*N*ames of mountains, mountain ranges, lakes, seas, rivers, volcanoes, etc.

It's almost too much to list what's covered here. Besides the above, it includes deserts, plains, marshes, bays, valleys, creeks, and any named location. Let's look at a few.

- Sahara Desert
- Gobi Desert

I'm going to stop right here. I happened to look both words up in *Merriam-Webster's*, both the collegiate and the unabridged versions; both had them listed as geographical entries. That wasn't surprising, though, because they are two of the bigger deserts in the world.

The green checks (✓) indicate they had an entry; the red *x*'s (✗) indicate they didn't.

✗ *Merriam-Webster Collegiate*
✗ *Merriam-Webster Unabridged*

✗ *American Heritage Dictionary*
✓ *Oxford English Dictionary*
✗ Dictionary.com
✓ Your Dictionary
✓ The Free Dictionary
✗ *Cambridge English Dictionary*
✓ Vocabulary.com
✓ Longman Dictionary
✗ *Collins Dictionary*

You may find a different situation when you go to look up smaller, lesser-known place-names. I looked up Cypress Creek, a (locally) well-known creek in the Houston area. I looked in the same dictionaries but couldn't find a listing.

Convinced that *Cypress Creek* must be listed somewhere, I continued checking and finally found it by doing a search on the internet, as well as finding it listed in Wikipedia, which had plenty of information about it as well as a map.

I wasn't surprised Wikipedia had an entry, but I was surprised that not one of the dictionaries I checked had it listed. I think the creek is about fifty miles long, so it's not that small. (To be fair, the Free Dictionary had a listing under its Widipedia section.)

This is just the reason why a book such as this is necessary. Now on with a few more examples.

- the Nile River
- the Lower Nile
- the Amazon River
- Lake Erie
- the Great Salt Lake
- Lake Huron

- the Pacific Ocean
- the Mediterranean Sea
- Cypress Creek
- Mount Olympus
- Mount Kilimanjaro
- San Juan Hill
- Mt. Etna
- Miller's Stream
- Black Sea

The list could go on to include thousands of names, which would be almost impossible to list here, but if you follow the rule regarding how a topographical area is named, you'll have no trouble with the capitalization.

And just like the importance of a job title doesn't matter when it comes capitalization, the size of the topographical area doesn't either. "Jasper's Crossing" and "Sally's Meadow" get the same treatment as the "Asian Continent" or the "Pacific Ocean."

Man-made structures

There are too many to list, but I think you'll get the idea. Any man-made structure that has been given a name, you capitalize. This category should be easier to check with dictionaries.

- Mount Rushmore
- the Brooklyn Bridge
- the Washington Monument
- the San Jacinto Monument
- Stonehenge
- the Walt Whitman Bridge
- the Delaware Memorial Bridge

- the New Jersey Turnpike
- the Statue of Liberty

But be careful regarding what you look up. For example, I couldn't find "Caribbean Islands" in many of the dictionaries I checked, but I found "Caribbean Island" in a few places. Also, "Gulf Stream" was capitalized (both words) in most of the dictionaries, but Vocabulary.com had it listed as "Gulf stream" with a lowercase *s*.

Going back a moment to islands: "Caribbean Islands" wasn't listed a lot of places because it is not the name of a specific geographical point; it refers to a group of islands in the Caribbean Sea, but "Caribbean Island" is capitalized because there is an island by that name. (The same reasoning applies to "Caribbean Sea.")

Street names

When referring to a street, capitalize its name (including the type of thoroughfare).

- University Avenue
- Baynard Boulevard
- Broom Street
- Clayton Road
- DuPont Parkway
- County Road 17
- FM 1960 (farm to market road)

As a side note, when citing addresses, spell out *avenue*, *boulevard*, *street*, *road*, etc., unless you cite an actual numbered address, then the abbreviated name may be used.

- University Avenue

- 5512 University Ave.
- Baynard Boulevard
- 1265 Baynard Blvd.
- Broom Street
- 4421 Broom St.
- Clayton Road
- 1022 Clayton Rd.

Chapter Six

POLITICAL DIVISIONS

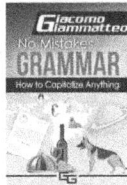

*P*olitical divisions of the world and more
(continents, countries, regions, states, provinces,
counties, etc.)

We've already discussed some of this.

When you refer to the Northeast, the West Coast, East Texas, or the South as specific areas and not just generalized compass directions, those regions are capitalized. And though I used the United States almost exclusively for examples, this reasoning applies to the entire world. (The list below includes volcanoes, mountain ranges, and deserts.)

- South America
- the Appenines
- Mt. Vesuvius
- Germany
- the Carpathians
- Chile
- the Atacama Desert

- the Kalahari
- South Africa
- Singapore
- Southeast Asia
- Eastern Europe
- the South Pacific

And once again, it doesn't matter how important or how big the locations are. Sulphur Springs, Texas deserves to be capitalized as much as London, England or Rome, Italy.

Be cautious of generalities, though; political divisions, much like job titles, are easy to mix up. That also includes legislative bodies, such as city councils, governing entities and buildings and landmarks.

- The city council will meet tonight to decide on the budget.

In that sentence, *city council* could be referring to any city council. But if you said "The Richmond City Council will meet tonight," then it would be capitalized as below:

- "The Richmond City Council will meet tonight to decide on a budget."

Below is what AP stylebook had to say.

Capitalize Capitol and City Hall when referring to a specific building: the U.S. Capitol, the Capitol, the Virginia Capitol, the state Capitol, Richmond City

Hall, City Hall ... Lowercase general references: You can't fight city hall.

— AP STYLEBOOK

When referring to a specific building, capitalize it.

- "The Texas State Capitol building in Austin is taller than the Capitol in Washington; in fact, it is the largest capitol building in the country."

There are several things to note in that sentence. First, take note that *building* isn't capitalized following "Texas State Capitol." *Building* is not part of the title. And "largest capitol building" is not capitalized because "capitol building" is describing the type of building, not a specific one.

Let's look at a few more examples.

- Sam has been a voting member of the Philadelphia City Council for more than ten years.
- Sam isn't here. The city council is meeting to decide on school districts.
- The Budget Committee nixed the "Walk to Stay Thin" project for this month.
- Will has been a senator for twenty-one years.
- Senator Will McMahon has held that office for twenty-one years.
- The committee on water rights has made a decision.
- The Bernadino Water Rights Committee has made a decision.

Notice the capitalization of "Walk to Stay Thin" in the sample sentence above. If an organization has named their campaign, it is capitalized (much like a named document is capitalized).

*L*ooking at governing entities again—if the words *city*, *county*, and *state* are being referred to in a legal document, and they indicate a specific entity as opposed to a region, capitalize them.

- The woman's paycheck was issued by the City of Los Angeles.
- She rides the bus every day to the city of Los Angeles.

In the first example, the "City of Los Angeles" is the entity who writes her check, her employer. In the second example, the "city of Los Angeles" is simply a place she rides the bus to (somewhere in the city).

During courtroom proceedings, you often hear the words "the State rests its case." In an instance like that, where *State* or *City* or *County* are used in place of a named entity, as in a lawsuit or other document, they are capitalized because they are being substituted for the actual name. If this were happening in California, "the State rests its case" would be no different than saying "California rests its case."

However, you would say "There are a lot of redwood trees in the state of California."

If any of those common words are part of the name, capitalize them. Some examples are the following.

- Salt Lake City
- the County Line restaurant
- Washington State
- the Empire State (nickname for New York State)
- Jersey City
- Kansas City
- the Windy City (similar to a nickname)
- Texas City

Capitalize any word of importance that is part of a proper noun.

- the Napoleonic Empire
- the Commonwealth of Australia
- the Republic of Georgia
- the United Kingdom
- the Fifth Republic (France)
- the Third Reich (Germany)
- the Northwest Territory
- the New England States
- the Fourth Ward (Houston)
- the Fifteenth Precinct

When using plurals to designate such groups, lowercase.

- The Trenton and Philadelphia city councils are meeting in separate rooms, even though they are discussing identical issues.

But if you used the words as part of the name, you'd capitalized them.

- The Philadelphia City Council and the Trenton City Council are meeting in separate rooms, even though they are discussing identical issues.

Much like the earlier example where *finance* wasn't capitalized because the name of the department was "Financial Control," the capitalizing of governmental bodies is similar. The governing body may function just like a city council, but its name may be different. It may be called the "Houston City Commission" and not the "Houston city council."

And don't get the impression we're only speaking of city councils. The San Francisco Housing Authority or the Phoenix Animal Rights Committee are capitalized just like the others.

The United States is often referred to simply as "the States," as in "I've been traveling for months, but next week I'm going back to the States."

In a situation like that, *States* is capitalized.

Part Three

SCHOOLS, COLLEGES, ACADEMIC DEGREES AND COURSES

Your alma mater may be a venerable institution to you, but it doesn't get any special treatment. It has to follow guidelines for what is and isn't capitalized.

Chapter Seven

SCHOOLS, COLLEGES, AND UNIVERSITIES

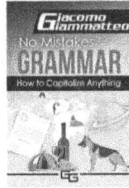

This is an easy one to master. All the words of importance in the name of educational institutions should be capitalized.

- Harvard University
- Temple University
- Boston College
- State University of New York (SUNY)

You capitalize them even if the words *university* or *college* are omitted.

- Stanford
- Yale
- Harvard
- Caltech

- A & M

Words like *of* do not need to be capitalized, so you would have the following:

- The University of Texas
- The University of Pennsylvania

In the next chapter, we'll deal with the more difficult chore of how to capitalize courses and degrees.

Chapter Eight

CAPITALIZATION OF ACADEMIC DEGREES

*I*f you look at most résumés or, for that matter, most business documents where degree information is included, you may think that damn near everything is capitalized, but it shouldn't be.

There is a fairly rigid yet simple system to follow. Let's take a look.

The Chicago Manual of Style recommends writing academic degrees in lower case except when directly preceding or following a name. A couple of example sentences follow:

✓ Marcus went to A&M to get a bachelor of science in mechanical engineering.

✗ Marcus went to A&M to get a Bachelor of Science in Mechanical Engineering.

✗ At the graduation party, Marcus introduced us to Jan Harris, Master of English Literature.

✓ At the graduation party, Marcus introduced Master of English Literature Jan Harris.

☑ At the graduation party, Marcus introduced us to Jan Harris, who mastered in English literature.

Notice in the last example how we didn't list Jan's degree as part of her name, simply that she studied in that area—that's why it wasn't capitalized.

Associated Press differs from CMOS in how to handle the listing of degrees. Like CMOS, they recommend keeping the shortened names of degrees, such as *bachelor's, master's,* or *doctorate,* in general lower case, but they recommend capitalizing them when spelled out in entirety—Bachelor of Science, Master of Fine Arts, Doctor of Philosophy—and they recommend doing this regardless of whether the degree precedes or follows the name. A few more examples may help

AP Style

☑ Marcus's intention was to get a Bachelor of Science degree in mechanical engineering, but now he's considering staying to obtain a master's degree.

☑ Jan gladly accepted her master's degree.

When it comes to abbreviating degrees, the two guides also differ on the use of periods.

Both recommend capitalizing (BA/B.A., M.A./MA, MS/M.S., PhD/Ph.D). CMOS suggests leaving the periods out unless consistency demands they be used, while AP suggests keeping the periods.

As mentioned, CMOS allows that it is okay to:

Capitalize degrees on business cards, on diplomas, or when displayed in a directory or resume. Lowercase them in running text, where they are almost always generic in nature.

CMOS
☑ John Asher, BS Economics (on a business card)
☑ Stanford University, Palo Alto, CA, BS Economics (on a résumé).

✖ Dear Mr. Marsh: I am interested in the position you advertised for director of finance and I feel my BS in Economics will be an advantage.

So if you're writing a cover letter inquiring about a job (as above), you follow the rules of keeping things lowercase (mostly). However, on a résumé, when listing the education, capitalization is acceptable.

Back to listings of degrees
I strongly recommend adhering to the style guide you selected to follow. Below are a final few examples.

- They have selected Marcus as the speaker tonight, despite him holding a Bachelor of Science degree only.

AP recommends capitalizing it this way, but CMOS suggests "holding a bachelor of science degree."

- Jan Harris, M.A., is doing an internship with Random House this summer.

AP would recommend this capitalization as well as this punctuation (periods included), but CMOS would omit the periods.

- After five years in industry, Jan decided to return to college, and she got her doctorate in literature.

Both guides would agree with the above.

Capitalizing courses

The following were taken from actual cover letters:

- I earned my BA in Economics from California State, Fullerton, CA.
- I achieved a BS in Economics from Penn State, University Park, PA.
- While lettering in football, I earned a BS in Mechanical Engineering from Texas A&M University, College Station, Texas.
- I maintained a 3.7 GPA while earning an MFA in Creative Writing from the University of Texas, Austin, Texas.

Which of these degree listings is right?

None of them. Remember, CMOS makes allowances for business cards and résumés, but not cover letters.

Look below to see the way they should be listed.

- BA economics, California State, Fullerton, CA
- BS economics, Penn State, University Park, PA
- BS mechanical engineering, Texas A&M, College Station, Texas
- MFA creative writing, University of Texas, Austin, Texas

The proper listing of degree majors is to capitalize only proper nouns:

- BA English literature
- BA Spanish (proper noun)
- BS accounting
- MFA creative writing

College Degrees

Perhaps you took English Literature (title of class) but you earned a degree as a master of fine arts in creative writing. Or you may have taken Accounting 101, but your degree was a B.A. in economics or finance.

Remember, academic degrees are not capitalized when spelled out.

- A bachelor of arts in Spanish
- A master's in economics
- A bachelor of science in petroleum engineering
- An MBA in finance
- A master of business administration in finance
- A doctoral degree in psychology
- A doctorate in chemistry

One more thing to discuss is the rampant overcapitalization of job skills found in business, especially on résumés. I know we touched on this, but the problem is so bad I feel we should at least mention it again.

Phrases like the following are often found in objectives and summaries:

✗ Experienced Team Leader and Project Manager with International experience and excellent Organizational Skills in putting together a Successful Management career. (This was on the résumé of a director from the medical-device industry)

The correct way to write that would be:

☑ Experienced team leader and project manager with international experience and excellent organizational skills in putting together a successful management career.

In other words, nothing but the initial *E* (which started the sentence) should have been capitalized.

I'll say this one more time about degrees because I see as many mistakes there as I do on objectives and summaries.

Presume the following was in a letter to an employer.

✖ In college, I Majored in Mechanical Engineering and minored in Electrical Engineering. I graduated with a Master of Science in Mechanical Engineering.

☑ In college, I majored in mechanical engineering and minored in electrical engineering. I graduated with a master of science in mechanical engineering.

School subjects are (not capitalized)

Despite what you may think or even what you think you remember, school subjects are not capitalized:

- algebra
- art
- English
- geography
- geology
- history
- math
- Spanish

*E*nglish and Spanish are capitalized because the names derive from proper nouns. The rest of the subjects are not. However, the titles of actual courses are capitalized. So, in high school, you may have enrolled in the following.

- Algebra 101
- American History
- Spanish II
- World Geography

Part Four

HISTORICAL EVENTS, NAMED DOCUMENTS, AND WORKS OF ART

This section deals with a lot of words that often leave people scratching their heads.

- Do you capitalize the name of the employee handbook?
- Is the name of that battle capitalized?
- Which words of that book or film title get capitalized?

Read on to find out.

Chapter Nine

HISTORICAL EVENTS

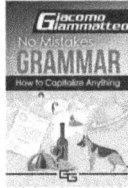

*I*f an event (or a day) is significant enough to have received a name, it is significant enough to be capitalized:

- the Battle of Hastings
- the Battle of Zama
- the Napoleonic Wars
- World War II
- the Revolutionary War
- Easter
- Christmas
- Bull Run
- Napoleon
- Caesar
- Thanksgiving
- Little Big Horn
- the Battle of the Alamo
- Great Depression

- the Renaissance
- Groundhog Day
- Halloween
- Waterloo

Remember, more than the proper noun gets capitalized. If the word is used as an adjective, it gets capitalized.

- He was a *Renaissance* man.
- Being short may have brought on a *Napoleonic* personality.
- He had a *Machiavellian* philosophy about business.

Some words, however, have slipped into lowercase usage. A few examples of both capitalized (eponyms) and lowercased events are found in the next chapter.

Periods of time

When referring to decades or to centuries as periods in history, they are usually not capitalized unless they have been given a specific name.

- That vase is a 5th-century piece from China.
- The '60s were a generation of experimental types.
- Al Capone lived during the *Roaring Twenties*.

Other named events

Events don't have to be considered historical to be capitalized. Other named events earn the capitalization right also.

- Academy Awards
- Italian-American Day
- the World Series

- the Stanley Cup Playoffs
- Gymnastics World Championship

With Hyphenation

When you have a hyphenated word that's capitalized, capitalize only the initial word—unless what follows is a proper noun. And if the second word is a proper noun, don't capitalize the prefix unless it is a proper noun.

- post-Nixon
- Italian-American
- pre-Caesar
- German-speaking people
- Twenty-third Avenue

Chapter Ten

EPONYMS

*E*ponyms present a unique problem. Many are capitalized, but many have moved to lowercase status. The worst, though, are the ones caught in between, where some dictionaries list the word one way and others the opposite. Another problem is when the word is capitalized, or not, depending on usage. Let's look at a few.

- herculean (mixed)
- Caesarean (mostly capitalized)
- satanic
- laconic (mostly lowercase)
- quixotic
- Shakespearian
- mercurial (mixed, more lowercase)
- draconian (mixed, more lowercase)
- Waterloo (mixed, mostly capitalized)

Regarding the above words, while some dictionaries capitalize *herculean*, some lowercase it. As far as *draconian*, about half the sources I checked had it lowercase. *Caesarean* was listed as uppercase in most dictionaries, although a few (*Longman* and *American Heritage*) had it as lowercase. A few had it lowercase but mentioned it was often capitalized. Some had it lowercase if used to refer to a "caesarean section" but uppercase if meaning "of or having to do with Julius Caesar." Many dictionaries also had it spelled as "cesarean section" (c-e-s) with "caesarean section" (c-a-e-s) listed as a variant.

Some sources also said to capitalize *Waterloo* when referring to the battle but to lowercase it when referring to any "disastrous defeat or reverse."

Merriam-Webster's says if a proper adjective has come to be used in a common form (such as *satanic* or *draconian*), it should be lowercased.

AP (Associated Press) has this to say regarding *eponyms*.

"Capitalize words that are derived from a proper noun and still depend on it for their meaning," such as *Shakespearean, Marxist,* and *Freudian*. "Lowercase words that are derived from a proper noun but no longer depend on it for their meaning," such as *herculean, caesarean,* and *malapropism*.

Examples of eponyms that are not capitalized include:

- **draconian** (from the Athenian lawmaker Draco)
- **mercurial** (from the Roman god Mercury) – rapid and unpredictable, especially in the changing of mood

- *quixotic* (from the fictional character Don Quixote) – foolishly impractical, especially in the pursuit of ideals
  - *satanic* (from Satan) – evil; fiendish

— AP (ASSOCIATED PRESS)

Not only do dictionaries disagree on the capitalization of eponyms, spellcheckers are notorious for flagging words like lowercase *french fries*; in fact, as I typed this, Microsoft Word's spellchecker automatically capitalized *French* and I had to go back and fix it.

I haven't seen an entry where *pasteurized* was capitalized, nor has any spellchecker flagged me for it. It looks as if that word has been fully assimilated, despite having derived from Louis Pasteur, the inventor of the process.

If you're not following a style guide, you could go either way on *herculean* or *french fries* and you'd have reliable sources to back you up, but *pasteurized* should be kept lowercase.

Of course, if you are following a style guide, stick to its recommendation.

If you question whether a word is lower- or uppercase, check your dictionary. Since some dictionaries don't have all the entries, if you have trouble finding the proper way to capitalize the word, err on the side of caution and keep it lowercase.

Below is a list of words derived from proper nouns but which are now lowercase in most instances:

- arabesque (made or done in the Arabic fashion).

- byzantine (from *Byzantium*, and listed as "often capitalized").
- epicurean (from the Greek philosopher Epicurus).
- italic (typically refers to the font formatting that resembles slanted handwriting—*like this*).
- laconic (from Lakonia)
- Lilliputian (referring to the island of Lilliput in Jonathan Swift's novel *Gulliver's Travels*).
- oedipal (relating to the *Oedipus complex* from *Oedipus* in Greek mythology).
- pyrrhic (from a battle that King Pyrrhus of Epirus fought with the Romans around 380 BC).
- spartan (of or relating to ancient Sparta). Often capitalized.
- utopian (having the characteristics of *Utopia*).

I've seen disagreement regarding a few of these words. *Byzantine*, for example, was capitalized in most dictionaries, but some sources said that if it is used to describe a personality trait or "complex or intricate system," it should be lowercased, but if it is referring to the Byzantine Empire or someone or something of that era, it should be capitalized.

Italic is another word that came with a qualifier. When referring to the font style resembling handwriting, it was always lowercased, but when used to refer to something related to ancient Italy, it was capitalized.

Lilliputian was a word that was usually capitalized despite several style guides advising to lowercase eponyms of fictional characters when used as adjectives (similar to *quixotic*).

Oedipal was a mixed bag. Half the dictionaries had it capitalized.

Laconic derives from a region and a people. Here's what Etymology Online has to say:

>The Greek term for an inhabitant of the ancient region of Laconia, in the southern Peloponnese, and of its capital Sparta, was Lákōn. The Spartans were renowned for not using two words where one would do (there is a story that when Philip of Macedon threatened invasion with 'If I enter Laconia, I will raze Sparta to the ground', the Spartans' only reply was 'If'), and so English used the adjective laconic (from Greek Lakōnikós) for 'sparing of speech'.

Spartan is the other word that is used similarly to *laconic* though *Spartan* may also be used to refer to bravery or courage or a sparse existence (using only the necessities). When using *Spartan*, you'd have to look at the context.

- I wouldn't argue with him; he has a *Spartanlike* disposition.
- He packs his own lunch, drives an old car, and lives a *Spartan* lifestyle.
- If you ask her a question, don't be surprised if her answer is *Spartan*.

You could substitute *laconic* in the third example, but not the first or second.

I was surprised by *Spartan*. I would have expected it to be capitalized everywhere, but about half the dictionaries had it lowercased.

Utopian was found capitalized in only two sources, but *Utopia*, the word it derives from, was capitalized.

With all of these words, if you look in enough dictionaries, you're likely to find differences. My suggestion, as always, is to pick a resource and stick with it.

As you see, eponyms present a problem unlike most ordinary words. Many of these words have been assimilated into the language and are lowercased: e.g., *italic*, *satanic*, *angelic*, and others.

Those words don't usually present an issue because they are always, or almost always, lowercased. The words that present a problem are those that are capitalized when used to mean "of, or having to do with" the original word but are lowercased when used as a general adjective.

Remember, we said that if a person or thing is given a name, it is usually capitalized. That doesn't just apply to real people. Characters in books, like Edmund Dantes from *The Count of Monte Cristo*, are capitalized, as well as Harry Potter, Batman, and Superman. Just because they're not real doesn't mean they don't deserve to be capitalized.

The same applies to characters in children's books: Henny Penny, Lil' Red Riding Hood, and Goldilocks are all capitalized, but the capitalization would only apply to the usage when it refers to the character, not the traits implied. A *henny penny* refers to someone who constantly worries or easily panics, as in "She's an old henny penny." And *goldilocks* means "an optimal balance," especially when referring to temperature, as in, "It's not too hot and not too cold."

So if you said, "Nelson climbs like he can grip the walls; he's a spider man," in that case, "spider man" is lowercased because you are referring to any spider man, but if you said, "Nelson climbs like he's Spider Man," it would be capitalized because you're comparing him to *the* Spider Man.

Not capitalizing words that require uppercase is almost as bad as overcapitalizing.

Chapter Eleven

DOCUMENTS AND WORKS OF ART

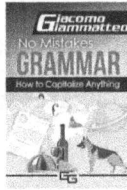

*N*amed documents, (often historical documents) are capitalized:

- the Constitution
- the Magna Carta
- the Declaration of Independence
- Treaty of Paris (there have been several)
- Treaty of Verdun

Along with historical documents, corporate documents (that are named) join the ranks.

If your company has an employee handbook, and it's titled "Employee Handbook," you need to capitalize it when it's specifically referred to.

- I read the *Employee Handbook* last night. It said nothing about dating co-workers.

- All *employee handbooks* are like that, but try to date someone, and you'll catch hell.

In the first instance, you are referring specifically to the handbook created by your company and titled "Employee Handbook." In the second, you are referring to a random employee handbook.

Capitalize any specific (named) document. If you write a paper that proposes a sales strategy for new phone and you title it "New Phone Sales Strategy," it would be capitalized when referred to as such, but only when you are referring to that document.

- What is our sales strategy for new phones?
- Where is the *New Phone Sales Strategy*? I want to read it.

If the operations director wrote a manual for increasing yields and he titled it "How to Increase Production While Increasing Yields," it would be capitalized when referred to by that name.

Chapter Twelve

WORKS OF ART

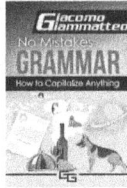

"**W**orks of art" covers a lot of territory. Ancient masterpieces, such as *David,* or the *Madonna,* the *Mona Lisa*, and the *Sistine Chapel* certainly qualify, but so do thousands of other things, such as those listed below:

- books
- movies
- songs
- poems
- paintings

And though many people may not think of the following as works of art, they technically are, and they fall under the same capitalization guidelines.

- magazine articles
- newspapers
- plays

In the broadest sense, what's considered a work of art is subjective, depending on how it is viewed. Technically, your five-year-old child's drawing may qualify as a work of art to you. And if you gave that drawing a name, it would be capitalized just like a famous sculpture of Moses.

There are guidelines regarding how to format works of art. Some sources recommend italics, and some recommend wrapping them in quotation marks, but the one thing that is consistent is the capitalization. All are capitalized. A few examples follow:

- The Godfather
- On Golden Pond
- Game of Thrones
- Who Let the Dogs Out?
- The Washington Post
- The Good, the Bad and the Ugly
- The Houston Chronicle

By "how to capitalize," I mean which words get initial caps and which don't. Different style guides have different recommendations, and for that reason, and to keep it simple, I like the rule to capitalize everything but the following words:

- a
- an
- and
- at
- but
- by
- for
- in

- nor
- of
- on
- or
- out
- so
- the
- to
- up
- yet

That's the simplest, easiest guideline I found. Other rules deal with parts of speech, the length of the words, etc. The only exception this rule has is the following.

Capitalize any word that occurs first or last in the title. An example would be "Who Let the Dogs Out?" shown above.

According to the rules *out* is one of the words not usually capitalized, but since it occurs as the last word, it is.

There is one other time that a few of the words may be capitalized. I'll let *Chicago* show the rule.

---

1. Lowercase prepositions, regardless of length, except when they are used adverbially or adjectivally (*up* in *Look Up*, *down* in *Turn Down*, *on* in *The On Button*, *to* in *Come To*, etc.) or when they compose part of a Latin expression used adjectivally or adverbially (*De Facto*, *In Vitro*, etc.).

— CMOS

When to Capitalize *The*

In the list above, I listed "The Washington Post" and "The Houston Chronicle," but should they have been "the Washington Post" and "the Houston Chronicle"?

Once again, it depends on which style guide you adhere to. CMOS recommends lowercase, even if "the" is part of the name, as it is in "The New York Times" and "The Boston Globe."

The two primary style guides differ in how you write the following:

AP

- I got a book reviewed by *The Boston Globe* today.
- Ralph got caught swindling; it was on the the third page of *The New York Times.*

CMOS

- I got a book reviewed by the *Boston Globe* today.
- Ralph got caught swindling; it was on the the third page of the *New York Times.*

There are times though, when you may omit *the* altogether. Consider the following:

- I did my modeling show on Friday. We got *New York Times* front-page coverage.
- After selling 100,000 books, Jennie became a *New York Times* best-selling author.

Part Five

ABBREVIATIONS, ACRONYMS, AND INITIALISMS

The world adopts new abbreviations every day. Thousands exist, and while you may be familiar with ones like FBI, CIA, NATO, and NASA, you may have forgotten some of the early acronyms, such as *laser*, *amphetamine*, and *radar*.

This section will show you how to deal with these types of words, whether abbreviations, acronyms, or initialisms.

Chapter Thirteen

ACRONYMS

*T*his chapter is almost a duplicate of one I wrote for *Simply Put: The Plain English Grammar Guide.* Initialisms and acronyms needed to be addressed in that book, but they also have a lot of capitalization issues, so I'm including them in this book as well. You might think all acronyms are capitalized, but as with most rules, there are always exceptions.

One of the exceptions is a well-established acronym: *laser.* It stands for "light amplification by stimulated emission of radiation," and it is spelled without capitals. Like most acronyms, it is pronounced using the first letters of the words those letters stand for to create a new word.

Both acronyms and initialisms are abbreviations, but there is a difference between the two. An acronym is an abbreviation formed by using (usually) the first letters of each word in the term—and they usually form a word, as in RAM (random access memory) or laser (light amplification by stimulated emission of radiation), but an initialism, while formed the same way, does not have to form a word:

- FBI (Federal Bureau of Investigation)
- CIA (Central Intelligence Agency)

Note how in these examples you say the word by using the initials: "F-B-I" or "C-I-A."

Style guides differ on whether to use periods after each letter, so I'll leave that up to you and your style guide.

One thing style guides agree on, though, is capitalization. Both acronyms and initialisms are to be capitalized—with a few exceptions (of course).

Initialisms and acronyms save a ton of time and effort. After all, it's easier to say "laser" than "light amplification by stimulated emission of radiation" and to say FBI than "Federal Bureau of Investigation."

Below are a few of the more common initialisms:

- ATM
- PIN
- ATCS (air-traffic-control system)
- SAT (scholastic-aptitude test)
- UPC
- ISBN
- HIV
- VIN

There are plenty more, but I think you get the point.

More on acronyms

To get one thing straight, I may refer to these abbreviations as either an initialism, an acronym, or an abbreviation.

It will depend on which we're talking about because all are abbreviations in one form or another.

The chart on the next page shows the relationship between the three.

Abbreviation (a shortening of a word)

Acronym (type of abbreviation. Usually uses initial letters or syllables of the words to form a new, pronouncible word)

Initialism (type of acronym. Uses initial letters from the words and uses them to form the "abbreviation." It is pronounced as individual letters.

As I said earlier, there are exceptions to the capitalization rule. Let's look at a few.

An initialism is a type of acronym that cannot be pronounced as a word and must be read letter by letter, like FBI or UCLA.

If you look up *acronym* in *Merriam-Webster's Collegiate Dictionary*, you get the following.

---

ac·ro·nym *noun* /ˈa-krə-ˌnim/

: a word (such as *NATO, radar,* or *laser*) formed from the initial letter or letters of each of the successive parts or major parts of a compound term; *also* : an abbreviation (such as *FBI*) formed from initial letters : initialism

— MERRIAM-WEBSTER COLLEGIATE

Note the end. "*An abbreviation (such as FBI) formed from initial letters: initialism.*"

Merriam-Webster is saying an *initialism* is an *acronym*. An *initialism* is formed from the initial letters, but an *acronym* may be formed from the *initial letter or letters* which is shown by the following words.

- radar
- Nabisco (National Biscuit Company)
- sonar

If you look up the words *sonar* and *radar* using OED, you'll see the information below, which is included in the word's *origin*.

- from so(und) na(vigation and) r(anging), on the pattern of radar.
- from ra(dio) d(etection) a(nd) r(anging).

And as you can see above, *Nabisco* is short for National Biscuit Company.

I think it's important to understand that initialisms, acronyms, and abbreviations are related. All involve the shortening of a word, or words, for brevity's sake. If it were me defining them, I'd say all initialisms are acronyms, which are all abbreviations.

Acronyms are a type of abbreviation, and initialisms are a type of acronym. Let's look at a few of the more common ones, though there are thousands to consider.

Abbreviations

- Dr. = doctor
- Mr. = mister
- exam = examination
- memo = memorandum
- decaf = decaffeinated
- lo-cal = low calorie

As you can see, abbreviations can be formed by using the first and last letters of a word, such as *doctor*, *mister*, *road*, etc.

Abbreviations can also include random letters, such as *blvd* for *boulevard*.

You should capitalize the abbreviation if the word would be capitalized in that use:

- She lives on a beautiful tree-lined boulevard.
- She lives on Baynard Boulevard
- She lives on Baynard Blvd.
- He always wanted to be a doctor.
- My cardiologist is Dr. Magnus.
- My cardiologist is Doctor Magnus.
- I forgot to tell you that Mr. Sharkey is my neighbor.
- I forgot to tell you that Mister Sharkey is my neighbor.

Acronyms

- NATO = North Atlantic Treaty Organization
- NASA = National Aeronautics and Space Administration
- scuba = self-contained underwater breathing apparatus
- radar = radio detection and ranging
- sonar = sound navigation and ranging
- GEICO = government employee insurance company

Acronyms are usually capitalized, but despite what some resources may tell you, they are not *always* capitalized. Once an acronym becomes accepted and used by the public, it doesn't take long to become part of the language. Consider the following, which many people have forgotten were originally acronyms.

- scuba
- radar

- sonar
- laser
- amphetamine

Amphetamine is short for its chemical name, a (lpha-) m (ethyl) phe (ne) t (hyl) amine.

Some acronyms are capitalized in the United States but may not be elsewhere. *NATO* and *NASA* are often seen in British English as *Nato* and *Nasa*.

Initialisms

- FBI
- CIA
- NBC
- CBS
- HBO

Abbreviations can sometimes form a word also, but the difference is an abbreviation is formed from only one word, as is shown in the examples of *exam*, *decaf*, and *memo* above, whereas an acronym uses letters from more than one word.

An initialism is formed from the letters of various words also, but they are pronounced as individual letters, such as

- FBI = "ef-bee-eye"
- NBC = "en-bee-cee"
- CEO = "cee-ee-oh"

Initialisms usually require the definite article *the* to precede them. You would say, "the FBI," "the NBA."

- *The* NBA has the best athletes.

- He's on *the* FBIs most-wanted list.
- *The* CIA operates internationally.
- *The* CEO wants to see you now!

But like most rules, there are exceptions. Consider HBO (Home Box Office). It is often heard without any article preceding it.

- Game of Thrones is shown on HBO.
- HBO has the best movies.
- I watched it on HBO.

Writing these examples brought up another thought. Pluralization of acronyms and initialisms. While you'll find style guides that offer various suggestions, I think the following works best.

Use a lowercase *s* and *do not* use an apostrophe when making a plural.

- Ten CEOs got together to discuss the situation.
- All the CFOs had to file their reports by mid-April.

However, if possession is implied, use an apostrophe.

- The mass murderer is on the FBI's most-wanted list.
- The NBA's salary cap was recently raised.

People use abbreviations, acronyms, and initialisms every day, and often without knowing what they stand for. We've already mentioned some like *scuba* and *radar,* but how about the following.

- A.M. (from Latin, *ante meridian*, meaning *"before noon"*)
- P.M (*post meridian*, meaning *"after noon"*)
- A.D. (*Anno Domini*, meaning *"in the year of our Lord"*)
- B.C. (before *Christ*)
- PDF (portable document format)

Corporations are big on acronyms whether it's for brand names or the name of the company.

- Nabisco (National Biscuit Company)
- 3M (Minnesota Mining and Manufacturing)
- Esso (Standard Oil)
- Sunoco (Sun Oil Company)
- OEM (original equipment manufacturer)

Going back to initialisms we can see that not all of them are capitalized. Consider the following.

- mph = miles per hour
- rpm = revolutions per minute
- mhz = megahertz

Technical terms are often capitalized differently, even as initialisms, so it's better to check your preferred dictionary or style guide.

Just when you think you've covered all the bases, another exception turns up. Consider JPEG, which might be considered part initialism, part acronym.

It is pronounced using the first letter *j* but the rest of it uses the remainder as a word. So it's *j-peg*.

Technology and the internet have added hundreds of

acronyms, including the ubiquitous LOL, BRB, PM, and more.

One you may not have thought of though is *CAPTCHA*, the code you need to type in for security purposes. It stands for "Completely Automated Public Turing" test and is used to tell "Computers and Humans Apart."

Or how about *Gestapo*? (it is an acronym for *Geheime Staatspolizei*—secret state police)

And of course, one of the major initialisms: USA.

Chapter Fourteen

INDIVIDUAL LETTERS JOINED TO WORDS

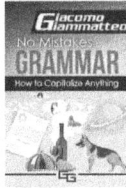

Capitalize individual letters when joined to words:

- T-shirt
- U-turn
- L-shaped
- A-frame

Anytime you need to use a word where an individual letter is joined to it, the letter is capitalized and a hyphen is added.

- The plumber said we needed a T-joint.
- We drove for miles before coming to the T-junction.
- It was an L-shaped object.
- Once we saw it, we made a U-turn.
- He wore a T-shirt to the wedding!

Notice in each of the sentences used as examples, the individual letter is capitalized.

Part Six

CAPITALIZING EDIBLES

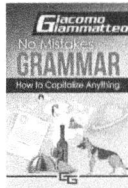

This section covers food groups as well as wine varietals and deals with a variety of capitalization issues related to these groups, not the least of which is the disagreement between style guides as well as the difference between style guides and dictionaries.

CMOS usually agrees with *Merriam-Webster's*; in fact, *Merriam-Webster's* is the dictionary CMOS recommends, but there are more than a few words they disagree on within food groups.

Chapter Fifteen

FOOD GROUPS

*Y*ou may not think so, but foods are one of the more difficult things to get right when it comes to capitalization. One of the reasons is because there is a lot of influence from adjectives formed from proper nouns. Consider the following and tell me which ones get capitalized and which don't.

- Waldorf salad
- Caesar's salad
- French dressing
- Bleu cheese dressing
- Cheddar cheese
- Brie cheese
- French fries
- Brussels sprouts

It almost doesn't matter what you guessed because you'd likely be able to find a reputable source to agree with you.

I got frustrated after finding more than a few disagreements, so I took the words above and looked them up in the following sources: *The Chicago Manual of Style*, Dictionary.com, *Merriam-Webster's* (collegiate and unabridged), the *Oxford English Dictionary*, and Vocabulary.com. The following table shows the results.

Word	CMOS (Chicago Manual of Style)	Merriam-Webster Collegiate and Unabridged	Vocabulary.com	Dictionary.com	OED (Oxford English)
waldorf salad	~ ~ ~	capitalized	capitalized	Capitalized	capitalized
Cheddar	Lowercase	Lowercase	capitalized	Lowercase	capitalized
Caesar salad	capitalized	capitalized	capitalized	capitalized	capitalized
French fry	Lowercase	Lowercase in both	Lowercase and hyphenated	capitalized or lowercase	capitalized
Bleu cheese	Lowercase	Lowercase	Lowercase	Lowercase	Lowercase
Swiss cheese	Lowercase	capitalized in Collegiate and not listed in other	capitalized	capitalized	capitalized
Brie cheese	Lowercase	capitalized	capitalized	capitalized	capitalized
Brussels sprouts	Lowercase	Lowercase, but Unabridged said "often capitalized"	lowercase	capitalized	capitalized

I checked a few more dictionaries after making that table, and to my surprise, I found that the *American Heritage Dictionary* had "Caesar salad" lowercased. And they had "cheddar" and "french fry" both lowercased and capitalized. The *Lookup* dictionary on my iPhone had "Caesar salad" lowercased.

CMOS

Quite a few dictionaries disagreed with each other, but

the surprising thing was that CMOS disagreed several times with *Merriam-Webster*, which is their recommend resource.

CMOS takes a firm stance on capitalization with foods. Take a look at what they have to say:

Personal, national, or geographical names, and words derived from such names, are often lowercased when used with a nonliteral meaning. For example, the cheese known as "gruyère" takes its name from a district in Switzerland but is not necessarily from there; "swiss cheese" (lowercase *s*) is a cheese that resembles Swiss emmentaler (which derives its name from the Emme River valley). Although some of the terms in this paragraph and the examples that follow are capitalized in *Webster's*, Chicago prefers to lowercase them in their nonliteral use.

anglicize

arabic numerals

arctics (boots)

bohemian

bordeaux

brie

brussels sprouts

burgundy

champagne

cheddar

delphic

diesel engine

dutch oven

epicure

frankfurter

french dressing

french fries

french windows

gruyère

herculean

homeric

india ink

italicize

italic type

jeremiad

lombardy poplar

manila envelope

morocco leather

pasteurize

pharisaic

philistine, philistinism

roman numerals

roman type

scotch (*but* Scotch whisky, a product of Scotland)

swiss cheese (not made in Switzerland)

venetian blinds

vulcanize

wiener

— CMOS (CHICAGO MANUAL OF STYLE)

As I've said many times, a writer needs to select a style guide and dictionary, then stick with it. You shouldn't jump from one to the other.

We've covered a few of the contentious foods, now let's look at some everyone seems to agree on.

Food is a hot topic nowadays, so capitalizing it correctly is taking on more importance. You can turn the TV on almost any time of day and find a show dealing with food. There's even a food channel.

The topic of food is so big that AP revised its style guide several years ago to include a new sixteen-page food section offering answers to style questions of various types.

Here are a few food examples that everyone agrees on.

- Golden Delicious apples
- Jerusalem artichokes
- Idaho potatoes
- Empire apples

Besides being brand names, several of these have part of their names derived from proper nouns. "Golden Delicious" is a brand, but Idaho potatoes, Jerusalem artichokes, and Empire apples are partially capitalized due to the proper nouns they derive from. *Empire* refers to the *Empire State* (New York).

Aside from brand names or being named for a proper noun, custom-named recipes are another reason for capitalization. Consider the following:

- Rick's Red Hot BBQ
- Kentucky Fried Chicken
- Oscar's Seafood Delight
- Pasquale's Pasta Supremo
- Tabasco sauce

named KFC (Kentucky Fried Chicken), it's capitalized, but if you are referring to chicken from Mama Jean's BBQ in Frankfort, Kentucky, it's simply Kentucky-fried chicken.

As far as Tabasco sauce, it is named after a state in Mexico.

If the name of the dish is not unique and simply describes what the dish is, it is lowercased. For example, if you said I had "blackened tilapia" for dinner, it is lowercased because many restaurants offer "blackened tilapia" as a menu item. If the menu item reads, "Carla's Special Blackened Tilapia," it earns uppercase letters.

If you're determined to find out whether a food should be capitalized, follow this process:

1. Is it a named menu item at a restaurant?
2. Is it a brand name? (like Red Delicious apples).
3. Is the name fully or partially derived from a proper noun?

If any of these conditions exist, at least part of the name should be capitalized.

If you can't determine that on your own, look it up in the dictionary, and if you get no results, resort to an encyclopedia or do a search on the internet.

Wines are another matter (a much more complicated one) which will be discussed in the chapter dealing with that subject.

With all capitalization, we stress capitalizing the name element or elements preceding the proper noun to preclude any confusion (discussed at length in "Dog Breeds," but with foods, I don't see any problem). That order of listing seldom occurs, and when it does, I don't see any potential for ambiguity. Take a look at the following:

- fettuccini Alfredo
- beef Stroganoff
- beef Wellington

Fettuccini is a type of pasta, and Alfredo is the name of the man who invented the dish. There is some disagreement on how beef Wellington got its name. Some claim it was from the Duke of Wellington, and some say it came from the town of Wellington, New Zealand.

Most other foods or dishes that derive their names from proper nouns have the proper noun first, as in Caesar salad or Waldorf salad.

Earlier I said AP had a new food section. The following is a partial list of some of the capitalized words:

From AP

- Alfredo
- Angus
- Asiago cheese.
- baked Alaska
- bananas Foster
- Beaujolais
- beef Wellington
- Belgian waffle
- Bennine
- Benedictine
- Bing cherries
- Black Forest cake
- BLT
- Bolognese
- Bordeaux
- Boston brown bread

- Boston cream pie
- Boston lettuce
- Brazil nut
- Broccolini
- Brussels sprouts
- Buffalo wings
- Bundt pan
- Burgundy
- Casear salad
- California roll
- Cavados
- Camembert
- Campari
- Canadian bacon
- Champagne
- Chianti
- Cobb salad
- Coca-Cola
- Cointreau
- Collins glass
- Cornish hen
- Crisco
- Crock-pot
- Danish pastry
- Dijon mustard
- Dr. Pepper
- Dungeness crab
- Dutch oven
- eggs Benedict
- Emmenthal
- English muffin
- Filet-O-Fish

- Fluffernutter
- French bread
- French dressing
- French toast
- General Tso's chicken
- GMO
- Gorgonzola cheese
- Grand marnier
- Grape-Nuts
- Greek salad
- Gruyere cheese
- Hass avocado
- Hereford
- IHOP
- India pale ale
- Instant Pot (or InstaPot)
- Irish coffee
- Jamaican jerk chicken
- Jamaican rum
- Jarlsberg cheese
- Kalamata olive
- Key lime
- Kobe beef
- Kool-aid
- Limburger cheese
- London broil
- Madeira
- Manhattan cocktail
- Manhattan clam chosder
- Marsala
- Marshmallow Fluff
- Mason jar

- McDonald's Corp.
- Meyer lemon
- Monterey Jack cheese
- Mornay sauce
- MSG
- Muenster cheese
- Negroni
- Neufchatel cheese
- New England clam chowder
- non-GMO
- Parmesan
- Parmigiano-Romano
- PB&J
- Peppadew
- Pepsi (Pepsi Cola)
- Philly cheesesteak (or Philadelphia cheesesteak)
- Pilsner
- Pizza Hut
- Popsicle
- Pyrex
- Reuben sandwich
- Rice Krispies
- Romano
- Roquefort cheese
- Russian dressing
- Salisbury steak
- Scotch whisky
- 7-Eleven
- 7UP
- Siracha sauce
- Swiss chard
- Swiss cheese

- Tabasco
- T-bone steak
- Tex-Mex
- Thai chilies
- Thai red curry paste
- Thousand Island dressing
- Tiki bar
- Toll House cookie
- Turkish delight
- Waldorf salad
- Wonder bread
- Worcestershire sauce
- York peppermint patties

Chapter Sixteen

LIST OF WINE VARIETALS

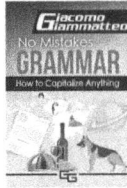

ost people think they know how to spell the names of wines, or at least the brands they drink. The problem is that they are often basing that knowledge on what they see written on the bottle. Wine merchants are like the American Kennel Club is with dog breeds or the Cat Fancier's Association is with cat breeds—they capitalize all the names.

However, wine varietals are no different than breed names when it comes to capitalization. Only the portion of the name derived from a proper noun (usually a geographic region) should be capitalized. I've listed two examples below, but the process will be dealt with in detail later.

- *Chianti* is a dry wine. (capitalized)
- When it comes to favorites, *brunello* is at the top of my list. (not capitalized)

The reasoning is simple: Chianti is a name derived from a

geographic region (Chianti), while *brunello* is simply a diminutive of *bruno* (*brown*).

Chicago, as well as many grammar purists, suggest only capitalizing the wine if it is actually produced in that region, so a Chianti grown in California, would be spelled "chianti", but I think expecting people to know where a wine is produced is asking too much.

For those of you who question the capitalization rules, think of wine varietals as wood. Wine comes from grapes, and wood comes from trees. You don't capitalize the tree names (oak, pine, mahogany, cherry), and you don't capitalize the grape names (unless either one derives the name from a proper noun).

You can see the capitalization in the following:

- A mahogany table
- A cherry desk
- An oak dresser
- A pine box

When you introduce a proper noun, however, it changes things.

- His house was built with Georgia pine.

Please notice two things about the last example. *Georgia* is capitalized because it derives from the state of Georgia. And *pine* is not capitalized because that's simply the type of wood —a common noun.

If you still have reservations about why capitalization works this way, consider the image below.

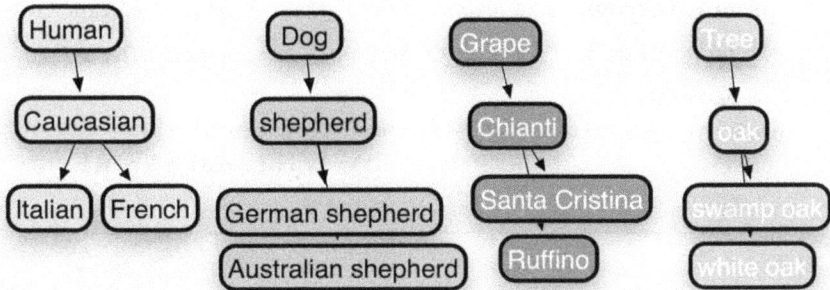

Wines

It would be a chore—a major one—to list all the wine varietals and their proper capitalizations, especially since new wines are continually being introduced, which would render the list useless. If it weren't for that, I'd tackle the challenge, but I doubt they're going to stop producing new wines, so we'll do this differently.

There are two ways to do this (as I see it). One is a method discussed years ago (1985) in an article by William Safire. I've included a link to a digital reprint the NYT (*New York Times*) did.

The gist of what Safire said is to capitalize a wine varietal if it is named after a region (proper noun) but *only* if the wine comes from that area. In other words, *chianti* would be spelled *Chianti* (capitalized) if it were produced near the Chianti region in Italy, however, if a chianti was made by a winery in Sicily (or anywhere else)), that wine would be lowercased.

I'll let Safire tell it in his own words:

When a wine is named for a place, and actually comes from that place, capitalize its name. Thus, the wine from the Burgundy and Bordeaux regions of France, as well as bubbly

from Champagne and brandy from Cognac - all real places,
shipping booze as if there were no tomorrow - the first letter is
uppercased.

— WILLIAM SAFIRE

Following the rules as Safire states would be difficult, and it would require more than a passing knowledge of wines and where they are produced; therefore, I have another suggestion. Capitalize the wines as Safire states (if named after a region), but don't worry if it is produced there or not. That would eliminate the possibility of having what appears to be inconsistencies, such as the examples below:

- Chianti produced in the Chianti region is spelled with a capital *C*.
- chianti from other regions is spelled with a lowercase *c*.

If you follow my advice, you won't run into this issue because all Chiantis, regardless of where they are produced, will be capitalized. The same rule would apply to all Bordeauxs and Burgundies and any other wine that would ordinarily require a capital letter.

In all matters dealing with grammar, one of the more important things is to be consistent, and I feel we should continue that policy with the capitalization of wines

I believe it would be too confusing to see Burgundy or Barolo spelled with a capital *B* when referring to a wine from those regions, and then to see it later with a lowercase *b* because it is produced somewhere else. That's why I propose to capitalize all wines of the same varietal, regardless of where they are produced. If Chianti or Barolo are supposed to be capitalized because they're named after a region, then capitalize them every time they're mentioned.

Now that we've gotten that over with, let's look at some wines that should be capitalized.

I can't go through a list of all known wines; there are too many. We can, however, list some of the common wines and show their capitalization requirements.

One more note: Ordinarily, I suggest checking the dictionary when in doubt; however, while researching, I did just that and was less than satisfied. I used *Merriam-Webster's*, Dictionary.com, and the *Oxford English Dictionary*, but each sometimes capitalized wines for no apparent rhyme or reason —wines that were not named after a region, town, individual, estate, or any proper noun I could find. At other times, they would list the wine as lowercased but with a note indicating that it was often capitalized.

For that reason, I suggest that if you need to look up a wine, use Google or search Wikipedia to determine where the wine originated or where it derived its name from. If it's a region, town, city, family name, or any proper noun, capitalize it; otherwise lowercase.

An example of what I'm referring to is seen in the screenshots below. The first is from *Merriam-Webster's* and the second from the *Oxford English Dictionary*, both dealing with cabernet sauvignon, though they list it as capitalized.

Cabernet Sau·vi·gnon *noun* \-ˌsō-vē-ˈnyōⁿ; -vən- yōn, -ˈyȯn, -ˈyän\ 🔊

: a dry red wine made from a single widely cultivated variety of black grape — called also *Cabernet*

Origin of CABERNET SAUVIGNON

French, from *cabernet*, a grape variety of the Médoc region + *sauvignon*, a grape variety of southwestern France, alteration of Middle French *sarvinien*

First Known Use: 1886

Merriam-Webster

Cabernet Sauvignon 🔊   f 🐦 G+ +

NOUN

1 A variety of black wine grape from the Bordeaux area of France, now grown throughout the world.

(+ Example sentences)

1.1 A red wine made from the Cabernet Sauvignon grape.

(+ Example sentences)

Oxford English Dictionary

Now look at cabernet sauvignon as it is displayed by *Merriam-Webster's Collegiate Dictionary*—it's lowercase. In the first example, using the unabridged version, it was uppercase.

cab·er·net sau·vi·gnon *noun,* /ˌka-bər-ˈnā-sō-vē-ˈnyōⁿ/ 🔊

: a dry red wine made from a single widely cultivated variety of black grape —called also *cabernet*

Origin of CABERNET SAUVIGNON

French

Merriam-Webster Collegiate Dictionary

And just to show you that *Merriam-Webster's* isn't playing around with wines only, here are two screenshots showing *Dalmatian*. One is from the *Merriam-Webster's* unabridged version and one from the collegiate version.

²Dal·ma·tian *noun* \()dal-ˈmä-shen\ 🔊

plural -s

1 : a native or inhabitant of Dalmatia

2 *or* **dalmatian** *also* **Dalmatian dog** *or* **dalmatian dog** : a large dog of a breed supposed to have originated in Dalmatia having a white short-haired coat with black or brown spots varying from dime to half-dollar size, standing from 19 to 23 inches high, and weighing from 35 to 50 pounds — called also *coach dog*

3 : a Romance language developed from colloquial Latin and extinct by the late 19th century that was spoken on the Dalmatian coast and Adriatic islands from Veglia to Ragusa

Merriam-Webster Unabridged

dalmatian *noun, often capitalized*

dal·ma·tian | \ dal-ˈmā-shən 🔊 \

Definition of *dalmatian*

: any of a breed of medium-sized dogs having a white short-haired coat with many black or brown spots

Merriam-Webster Collegiate

Back to the cabernet. I looked in numerous dictionaries and also checked with the Online Etymology Dictionary. Nowhere could I find a reason why it should be capitalized. Here is the listing from Etymology online:

---

cabernet (n.)

family of grapes, or wine made from them, 1833, from French. There seems to be no general agreement on the etymology; the word seems not very old in

French and is from the Médoc dialect. Supposedly the best of them, *cabernet sauvignon* is attested in English from 1846.

— ONLINE ETYMOLOGY DICTIONARY

I'll now list a number of currently produced wine varietals and their capitalization. Some of this list comes from Wines.com.

COMMON WINE TYPES

albariño: (not capitalized) from the Galicia region of Spain, so no capitalization.

amarone: (not capitalized) Mostly seen capitalized, but I don't know why. It doesn't seem to derive its name from a proper noun. Look at the origin cited by OED:

1960s; earliest use found in The New York Times Magazine. From Italian amarone from amaro bitter + -one, augmentative suffix.

— OED

Amarone translates to "*great bitter,*" referring to the bitter taste. The name *amarone* was given to it to distinguish it from a sweet wine of that region.

If it were me, I'd leave it lowercase to keep consistent.

arneis: (not capitalized) This comes from Italy's Piedmont (Piedmontese) region. I couldn't find this in many dictionaries. *Merriam-Webster* had the entry listed as capitalized but with the lowercased version as a variant.

I'd treat this the same as *amarone* and leave it lowercase, as I can find no reason to capitalize it.

It originated in the Piedmont region of Italy, and the name translates to "*little rascal.*"

Asti Spumante: (capitalized) Named after the village of Asti in Northern Italy. Once again, I'm baffled. I see why *Asti* is capitalized but why *Spumante Spumante* is simply a name for a bubbly, effervescent wine.

auslese: (capitalized) Name for a German wine meaning "selected harvest."

Barbaresco: (capitalized) Named after Barbaresco village in Northern Italy.

Bardolino: (capitalized) From *Bardolino*, village on Lake Garda, Italy

Barolo: (capitalized) Named after *Barolo*, a village in the Piedmont region, Italy

Beaujolais: (capitalized) Named after *Beaujolais* a region of central France

blanc de blancs: (not capitalized) The name describes the wine: literal translation is "white from whites."

blanc de noirs: *Merriam-Webster* lists it as lowercase but "often (capitalized)" I don't know why it would be (capitalized) The name is French for "white from blacks," and I couldn't find any reason for the capitalization.

Brunello di Montalcino: (capitalized) Named after the town of Montalcino in Italy. *Brunello* by itself would not be capitalized, so you might say, "I love a good brunello." However, in this example, it is the name of the wine and it is paired with the name of a town.

cabernet sauvignon: (not capitalized) It is named for

the grape, not a region. French, from *cabernet*, a grape variety of the Médoc region + *sauvignon*, a grape variety of southwestern France. More dictionaries than not had this capitalized, but I have no idea why. Some of the ones who had the entry capitalized, acknowledged it was often lowercased.

Carignan: (capitalized) Named after *Carignan*, a town near Bordeaux, France

carmenere: (not capitalized) Named after the grape and gets its name from the French word for crimson (*carmin*).

cava: (not capitalized) A sparkling wine from Catalonia, Spain.

charbono: (not capitalized) Italian white wine grown in the Savoie wine region.

Champagne: (capitalized) Named after the Champagne region of France.

While I say *capitalized*, the majority of dictionaries list the entry as lowercase. I've listed the origin as noted by *Merriam-Webster*.

Origin of CHAMPAGNE

French, from *Champagne*, region (formerly province) of northeastern France where it was first produced, from Late Latin *campania* level country

— MERRIAM-WEBSTER UNABRIDGED

The following is from the Online Etymology Dictionary.

champagne (n.) effervescent wine, 1660s, from French, short for *vin de Champagne* "wine made in *Champagne*," the former province in northeast France, literally "open country." Originally any wine from this region (especially from the vinyards [*sic*] south of Reims); the sense focused on the "sparkling" wines made there (the effervescence is artificially produced), then by late 18c. expanded to effervescent wines made anywhere.

— ONLINE ETYMOLOGY DICTIONARY

Note it lists the word as short for *vin de Champagne which translates to* "wine made in *Champagne*." As far as I'm concerned, that is plenty of justification for capitalizing.

As in all situations like this, if the word is used as a general descriptor, as in "It was a *champagne* type wine" or if you're referring to the color *champagne*, I'd leave it lowercased. But if referring to the wine, as in "I'll take some Champagne," I'd capitalize it. However, if you don't agree and want to leave it lowercased, there is plenty of justification from major sources.

chardonnay: (not capitalized) Originated in the Burgundy region of France.

Châteauneuf-du-Pape: (capitalized) Named after *Châteauneuf-du-Pape*, a commune near Avignon, France.

chenin blanc: (not capitalized)

Chianti: (capitalized) Named after the Chianti region in Italy.

Chianti Classico: (capitalized) See above.

claret: (not capitalized).

colombard: (not capitalized).

constantia: (not capitalized), although *Merriam-Webster* lists it as "often capitilized," probably due to its suspected origin from a former estate near Cape Town, Union of South Africa.

cortese: (not capitalized) (white wine grown in the Asti region of Italy).

dolcetto: (not capitalized) Name means "little sweet one," and it is grown in Italy's Piedmont region.

eiswein: (not capitalized) German for "ice wine." So called because the grapes are frozen while still on the vine.

Frascati: (capitalized) After the city of Frascati, southeast of Rome.

fumé blanc: (not capitalized) Fumé blanc is sauvignon blanc that is made in the United States.

Gamay: (capitalized) It is suggested the name derives from Gamay, a village in France. It is not capitalized in the *Merriam-Webster Unabridged* version, however, it carries a note that says it is "often (capitalized)"

Gamay Beaujolais: (capitalized) Since we capitalized Gamay and Beaujolais, I'm going to suggest we capitalize Gamay Beaujolais; otherwise it would be confusing.

gattinara: (not capitalized) A dark, red Italian table wine made from the nebbiolo grape.

gewürztraminer: (not capitalized) *Merriam-Webster* lists this as "often capitalized," however, it is a white from the Alsace region, and I can't see why it would require a capital.

grappa: (not capitalized) It is an Italian drink—more of a brandy—often added to coffee and consumed after meals or in the evening.

grenache: (not capitalized) Comes from a sweet red grape grown in the Liguria region of Italy. Also grown in Spain and France. At one time, it was the second most widely grown grape in the world. It is slipping in popularity, but remains in the top ten.

Johannisberg Riesling: (capitalized) From *Johannisberg*, castle and village in the Rheingau, Germany region. I understand why *Johannisberg* is capitalized, but I had to dig deep to find out why *riesling* was (capitalized)

It seems as if the name likely derived from a small stream and a small vineyard both called *Ritzling* in Austria. The stream and vineyard are claimed to have given *Riesling* its name.

lambrusco: (not capitalized) From Latin *labruscum* fruit of the wild grape *Vitis labrusca*.

Liebfraumilch: (capitalized) Named after a religious foundation in Germany, where the wine was first produced.

Madeira: (capitalized) A fortified wine named after the Madeira Islands (Portuguese).

malbec: (not capitalized) Produced heavily in Argentina.

Marsala: (capitalized) Named after the city of Marsala, Sicily. A sweet wine used in cooking: *veal marsala, chicken marsala*.

marsanne: (not capitalized) The grape most likely originated in the Rhône-wine region of France.

merlot: (not capitalized) From France. *Merriam-Webster* lists it as "often capitalized," but I see no reason why. It comes from the French *merle,* meaning *"blackbird."*

Montepulciano: (capitalized) Named after the town of Montepulciano in the Tuscany region of Italy.

moscato: (not capitalized) Named after the grape, not a region.

mourvedre: (not capitalized) A red wine grape variety that is grown in many regions.

Müller-Thurgau: (capitalized) Wine was created by Hermann Müller who was from the Swiss Canton of Thurgau.

muscat: (not capitalized) Named after the grape, which is used in many wines. Moscato derives its name from *muscat*.

nebbiolo: (not capitalized) Grown in the Piedmont region of Italy. The nebbiolo grape is used for the highly acclaimed Barolo and Barbaresco wines.

petit verdot: (not capitalized) From the Bordeaux region of France. It is used for blending with cabernet sauvignon.

petite sirah: (not capitalized) Mostly used as a blending wine.

pinot blanc: (not capitalized) A varietion of pinot noir.

pinot grigio/pinot gris: (not capitalized) Named after the grapes.

pinot meunier: (not capitalized) Grown in the Champagne region of France, it is often blended with other wines to add fruit flavors to Champagne.

pinot noir: (not capitalized) From a well-known, popular grape variety grown in Burgundy.

port: (not capitalized) A fortified wine from Portugal.

I'm going against the grain here, but I'd say it should be (capitalized) When the word's origin is looked up, I get the following.

Origin

Early 17th century: shortened form of Porto, a major port from which the wine is shipped.

— OED

Notice that it states "shortened form of Porto," which was the city where the wine shipped from.

Merriam-Webster's Collegiate Dictionary lists the origin as follows.

Origin of PORT
Oporto, Portugal

— MERRIAM-WEBSTER COLLEGIATE

If you adhere to William Safire's advice, I can see why *port* isn't capitalized as its name derives from the town where it was shipped, not necessarily the same region where it was grown and produced.

I think you could go either way with this one. You have reputable resources to back you up if you lowercase and logic to back you up if you capitalize.

rosé: (not capitalized) A mix of red and white wines. Often referred to as *blush*.

roussanne: (not capitalized) A white wine grape grown in the northern part of the Rhône Valley.

sangiovese: (not capitalized) Sangiovese is a grape used in many Italian wines, including Chianti.

sauvignon blanc: (not capitalized) A white wine made from the sauvignon grape.

sherry: (not capitalized) Fortified wine from the Jerez de la Frontera district in southern Spain.

Soave: (capitalized) Name from Soave, a village in Northern Italy.

Tokay: (capitalized) A sweet dessert wine made near the town of Tokaj, in Hungary.

Trebbiano: (capitalized) (Italian, perhaps from Latin *Trebulanus* of Trebula, from *Trebula*, an ancient town in Campania, Italy)

ugni blanc: (not capitalized).

Valpolicella: (capitalized) Named after *Valpolicella*, a valley of northern Italy

verdicchio: (not capitalized) *Merriam-Webster* lists it as "often (capitalized)" The name *verdicchio* derives from *verde* (or *green*). This is another name that I can't see a reason for capitalizing.

zinfandel: (not capitalized) *Merriam-Webster* once again lists this as "often capitalized," however, this time it cites a possible reason. *Merriam-Webster* says the name may derive from a European place name.

Summary

As you see, the decisions on whether to capitalize wine names is far from simple, and if you're not familiar with the wine's history, you may have to spend some time finding out where the wine was originally produced, or where the name came from. On the other hand, you could always keep it simple and opt to capitalize all wine varietals. If you do that, remember to be consistent.

I've included a note from Murmur.com that lists some of the more common wines that are *always* capitalized as well as those that are *never* capitalized (at least according to them).

A quick hit list for your convenience

Wines that are not capitalized because they're named for their grape of origin or another common noun.

Popular Reds

- shiraz or syrah
- petite syrah (not to be confused with the above)
- cabernet sauvignon
- petit perdot
- merlot (French, form of *merele* meaning "blackbird")
- pinot noir (French for "black pinecone," which describes the grapes)
- malbec
- tempranillo (diminutive of teprano, "early," in Spanish)
- All table wine, including vins de table (French), vino da tavola (Italian), vino de mesa (Spanish)

Popular Whites

- sauvignon blac (French for "wild white")
- riesling* (a German wine)
- chardonnay (fun fact: this varietal originated in Burgundy, France)
- pinot grigio or pinot gris

Other Popular Wines

port
    sherry
    rosé (a style of wine, red sparkling wine to be exact)

Wines that are for sure capitalized

- Chianti (region in Italy)
- Chinon (town in France, the wine is from this area)
- Champagne (but only if it's from the Champagne region of France)
- Lambrusco (Italian sparkling red)
- Cava (sparkling wine from Spain)
- Espumante (sparkling wine from Portugal)
- Asti (sparkling wine from Italy)
- Rioja (from the Rioja region in Spain)
- Burgundy (region in France)

Please note, as stated above, that if a wine is named for the grape, it's lowercased: cabernet sauvignon, chardonnay, malbec, merlot, pinots (any of them), riesling, shiraz, and zinfandel.

As stated earlier though, *riesling* is often capitalized due to the name suspected of deriving from a stream or winery in Austria. I think you'd be safe capitalizing this one. Most dictionaries capitalize it.

Note that we've been discussing the *type* of wine, not the name of the wine. The name of a wine—*Santa Cristina or Brunello de Montalcino*—is capitalized, but the *type* of wine Chianti or brunello is capitalized, or not, based on the above-stated rules.

And for your interest, below is a list of the top ten grape varieties in the world (according to an article in Forbes). By the way, I did not capitalize these wines—Forbes did—so I left them as they were.

1. Cabernet Sauvignon, 840,000 acres (340,000 hectares)
2. Merlot, 657,300 acres (266,000 hectares)

3. Tempranillo, 570,800 acres (231,000 hectares)
4. Airén, 538 700 acres (218 000 hectares)
5. Chardonnay, 518,900 acres (211,000 hectares)
6. Syrah, 470 000 acres (190,000 hectares)
7. Grenache Noir, 402,780 acres (163,000 hectares)
8. Sauvignon Blanc, 299 000 acres (121,000 hectares)
9. Pinot Noir, 285,000 acres (115,000 hectares)
10. Trebbiano Toscano/Ugni Blanc, 274,300 acres (111,000 hectares)

For reference, one hectare is equal to about 2.47 acres.

This list is by no means comprehensive. There are more than 10,000 types of grapes in the world, and the last estimate I saw put the number of wines at greater than 400,000. But this list should cover a lot of your capitalization questions, and for those we haven't touched upon, refer to Google or Wikipedia or another trusted source.

If you have questions regarding capitalization when it comes to cats, cattle, dogs, donkeys, goats, horses, poultry, sheep, or swine, check out the chapters dealing with that, where you'll find the names, not just rules.

Part Seven

MISCELLANEOUS

This section deals with capitalizing when using dialogue, as well as a few miscellaneous areas where words need to be capitalized, such as with brand names, ethnicities, religious references, celestial bodies, and more.

Chapter Seventeen

CAPITALIZING DIALOGUE

CAPITALIZING DIALOGUE
Punctuating Dialogue

Dialogue is a great way to get inside your protagonist's or antagonist's head. But some dialogue is done poorly. The wrong tags are used, the wrong punctuation, and the author either consistently uses a person's name or doesn't use the name enough. Then there's the problem I see too often—improper capitalization when using dialogue.

You wouldn't ordinarily capitalize the word *captain*, but if it began a sentence, you would, or if you referred to a person using *captain* as a title, such as "Captain Joseph Estelle was recently promoted."

But in dialogue, you would also capitalize *captain* if you were addressing the person even without their full name:

- Connie walked up the stairs. "Hey, Captain. How's it going?"

Connie could have just as easily said, "Hey, Coop [the captain's name]. How's it going?"

The same thing goes for your parents or anyone else. If you can substitute the person's name for the term, it is (capitalized) Below is another example.

- "Can I go to the mall, Mom?"

We capitalized *mom* because the boy could have just as easily said,

- "Can I go to the mall, Margaret?"

He may have gotten slapped in the face, but he could have said it and had it make sense.

On the other hand, if you said, "I'm going to the mall with my mom," no capitalization is necessary.

You couldn't comfortably substitute a name for *mom*. Try it.

- "I'm going to the mall with my Margaret."

See, it doesn't work.

That was easy, right? From now on, when writing dialogue, substitute the person's name and see if the sentence still sounds right. If it does, capitalize. If it doesn't, don't.

One more thing before we sign off. The picture below is how you would capitalize dialogue when someone is speaking to their mother. It's missing the quotation marks because there was more dialogue on both sides of it.

I'll be home late, Mom.

Terms Of Endearment

Terms of endearment aren't (capitalized) For example, let's say you call your husband "honey." I know it's unlikely unless you're a newlywed, but it could happen.

You may come home from work, smell food cooking, and say:

- "Thanks for the dinner, honey."

But you wouldn't call your mother and say,

- "When I got home, *honey* was already making dinner."

You don't capitalize *honey* in either case.

Nicknames Are Different.

Nicknames are substitutes for the real name to be used by anyone. One of the characters in my book *Murder Takes Time* is named Doggs. That's not his real name, but when people address him, they use his nickname.

- "Give me a smoke, Doggs."
- "Hey, Doggs, you got a smoke?"

Let's assume his real name was Tony. Now, substitute *Tony* in each of the examples above.

- "Give me a smoke, Tony."
- "Hey, Tony, you got a smoke?"

As you can see, it works perfectly.

Nicknames work the same way with other things, such as

companies or even geographic locations. Consider the following:

- the Big Apple (NYC)
- Big Blue (IBM)
- the Windy City (Chicago)

There are plenty of other punctuation rules related to dialogue, such as where to put commas, how to use question marks and exclamation points, the proper way to use quotation marks, and how to capitalize when the tag is in the middle of the dialogue. Let's take a look at that.

- "You *have* to go," Jane said, "or I'm not going either."
- "You *have* to go," Jane said. "If you don't, I'm not going either."
- "You *have* to go," Jane said. "But if you don't, I won't either."

Of the three, only the first is a clear example of a sentence interrupted and then continued with the same thought. Sentence two is definitely an example of two sentences (hence the capitalization). And example three could go either way:

- "You *have* to go," Jane said. "But if you don't, I won't either."
- "You *have* to go," Jane said, "but if you don't, I won't either."

*I*n an earlier example, when we used a personal pronoun (*my*) with *mom*, it affected the capitalization of that word.

Personal pronouns do that, so let's look deeper.

Capitalize titles when they refer to a specific person, *unless* they are modified by a personal pronoun. I'll give a few examples.

✗ I'm going to play ball with *my* Cousin Bobby.

✅ I'm going to play ball with Cousin Bobby.

✅ I'm going to play ball with *my* cousin Bobby.

✅ Uncle Johnny picks me up to caddy for him every Sunday.

✗ *My* uncle Johnny picks me up to caddy for him every Sunday.

Chapter Eighteen

OTHER THINGS TO CAPITALIZE

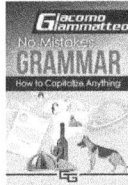

We've covered landmarks, man-made structures, works of art, and more. We didn't mention company names, but I think that's obvious; company names are no different than a person's name.

- Apple
- Google
- IBM
- Random House
- Merriam-Webster

Brand names of products from companies should also be capitalized unless the company chooses not to (usually for marketing reasons).

- Kleenex
- Q-tips
- Jet Ski

- iPod
- iPhone
- iPad
- iMac
- eBay

Four of the last five examples are Apple products.

Aside from those word types, there are the nationalities, languages, and ethnic groups, as well as adjectives derived from them.

- Caucasian
- Asian
- Chinese
- Russian
- Nigerian

Notice that all these derive from proper nouns: Caucasus Mountains, Asia, China, Russia, and Nigeria. However, you would not capitalize *black* or *white* when using those terms to refer to someone's ethnicity.

- He is a black person.
- He is a white person.
- She is black.
- She is white.

As mentioned earlier, the adjectives derived from those words are also (capitalized)

- Italian-American singer
- Irish golfer

- German soldier
- Australian sheepherder

Other things

You should always capitalize proper nouns and any words formed from them; do not capitalize common nouns. The following are the types of words you would usually capitalize:

- Names for the deity, religions, religious followers, sacred books – God, Buddha, Allah, Christianity, Muslims, Bible, Torah

Electronics and technology

With the advent of electronics, technology-fueled production has produced an abundance of new products and services.

When these products first appear, they are often capitalized, but as they become ubiquitous, the capitalization typically disappears with the novelty. A few examples follow:

- internet (some still capitalize it, but it's rapidly moving toward lowercase)
- web (same thing with *web* and related terms)
- world wide web
- website

Named software is another thing entirely. It is capitalized just like works of art or brand-name products. The following would all be capitalized:

- Adobe Software
- Microsoft Word

- Pages
- Portable Document Format (PDF)

Many people fail to remember the capitalization of words such as PDF, because those words are usually seen listed as .pdf, and in that format, they're (not capitalized) And, by the way, technically, you don't say "I'll send you a PDF" or "Can you send me a PDF?"

You'd say "I'll send you a PDF file" because PDF stands for "portable document format." Also, it is uppercase (PDF) when used as an initialism or spelled out in text (portable document format), just not when used as a file extension (.pdf).

Months and days are (capitalized) All months, January through December, and all days of the week, Sunday through Saturday, are (capitalized)

Seasons are not capitalized, so it would be *spring*, *summer*, *fall*, and *winter*.

Most of the style guides recommend writing dates using numbers only, not using the *st*, *nd*, *rd*, or *th* endings:

- July 30, 2001
- April 11, 2019
- July 4, 2002

AP recommends the following:

Our style is to abbreviate the month when used with a date, and to use the numeral in all uses: Nov. 3, Nov 8, Nov. 21. (The months March, April, May, June and July aren't abbreviated: March 2, April 27, June 21.)

———————————————————————————

According to AP, then, the following dates would be written with abbreviations.

- Nov. 11, 1988
- Dec. 22, 2011
- Jan. 14, 2015

Heavenly bodies

Don't capitalize the moon or the sun, but *do* capitalize the planets.

Depending on how you use it, *earth* is either lowercased or (capitalized) It is capitalized if you are referring to it as a planet, but not if you're speaking of the ground as earth.

All of the planets (except Earth) were named after Roman or Greek gods.

You would also capitalize any named heavenly body such as *Polaris, Sirius, the Milky Way Galaxy, the Alpha Centauri System, Antares,* etc. You wouldn't say, "I was digging through the Earth today" when referring to digging in the garden. You would only say that if you meant you were literally digging through the Earth, meaning the planet.

You would, however, say "Earth revolves around the sun." Or you would say, "Jupiter has sixty-three moons, and Earth has only one." (When *Earth* is preceded by the word *the* it is generally lowercased.)

Heavenly bodies: *Martian,* and *Venusian,* but *solar,* and *lunar* or *red planet* when referring to Mars. Also, named heavenly bodies are capitalized but only the portion dealing with a proper noun: *Halley's comet*. (*Merriam-Webster* didn't have this listed in either the collegiate or the unabridged version.) It was listed in the American Heritage Dictionary, Dictionary.com, Collins Dictionary, OED, and Webster's New World.

Medical and technical terms

If you are writing about technical issues, you will likely run across numerous instances where capitalization is needed. Often, an invention, product, discovery, or illness is named after the person who discovered or invented it or first contracted the disease. Such is the case with the following:

- Alzheimer's disease
- Lou Gehrig's disease
- Bunsen burner
- Petri dish

In addition to the above, scales of temperatures were named after people as well, so they need to be (capitalized)

- Kelvin
- Celsius
- Fahrenheit

When writing a temperature and spelling out the text, you would say "It's ninety-eight degrees Fahrenheit."

Some dictionaries had *Kelvin*, *Celsius*, and *Fahrenheit* lowercased or had it capitalized with lowercase listed as a variant, but for the most part, I think you're safe to capitalize.

Chemical elements are lowercased regardless of the origin of the name. So the following would be lowercased despite having derived from proper nouns: Pluto, Uranus, and California:

- plutonium
- uranium
- californium

Diseases and medical conditions are not capitalized unless the name is derived from a proper noun:

- Parkinson's disease
- Ebola virus
- West Nile virus
- Alzheimer's disease
- Lyme disease
- Crohn's disease

But the following would be all lowercase.

- diabetes
- cancer
- lupus
- multiple sclerosis
- tuberculosis

Prescription drugs are lowercased unless they are a brand name.

- aspirin
- Bayer Aspirin
- Lipitor
- a statin
- clopidogrel
- Plavix
- Levemir

- insulin

Plants are often in need of capitalization. With plants, follow the same rule as with other things: if the name or a portion of the name derives from a proper noun, capitalize that part of the name.

Finding the origins for plant names can be more difficult than for other things.

Most plant names are lowercased, but there are a few exceptions. Consider the following:

- Douglas fir
- Georgia pine
- California poppy

But it would be lowercased for the following.

- ponderosa pine
- bougainvillea
- live oak
- poinsettia

Despite bougainvillea and poinsettia deriving their names from people (Louis Antoine de Bougainville and Joel R. Poinsett), these plant names are (not capitalized) I don't know why that is, but if anyone questions you on it, you have multiple dictionaries to back you up.

Most single-word plant names you will find in the dictionary, but many of the plant names containing two or more words will not be listed. You may have to resort to an internet search.

Religions and names of deities

- Capitalize the names of the religion: Christianity, Judaism, Hinduism, Islam as well as Catholic, Jew, Muslim, Christian.
- Capitalize the *Bible*, but not biblical.
- Capitalize *Torah*, *Koran*, and *Vedas*
- Capitalize religious holidays: *Christmas, Easter, Hannukkah, Ramadan,* and *Holi.*
- Do not capitalize heaven, hell, the devil, or satanic.

The names that saints, prophets, and apostles are known as are (capitalized)

- St. John the Baptist (or just John the Baptist)
- the Madonna
- the Prophet

Recognized names of prayers or religious artifacts are (capitalized)

- the Hail Mary
- the Lord's Prayer
- the Ten Commandments
- the Ark of the Covenant
- the Shroud of Turin

Also capitalize the names of the following:

- Allah
- Almighty, the
- Buddha
- Christ
- Creator, the

- God
- Jehovah
- Messiah
- Mother Nature
- St. Gabriel the Archangel
- Zarathushtra

Do not capitalize *god* or *goddess* if used to refer to pagan deities, but do capitalize the names of those deities:

- Zeus was a god of ancient Greece.
- His wife was Hera.
- The planet Venus was named after the goddess Venus.

Capitalize *God* when using the word to refer to God, but not when referring to other things:

- Some sports stars are looked upon as modern-day gods.
- In the same vein, movie actresses are often seen as goddesses.

Curse words using God are kept lowercase as well.

- goddamn
- goddamnit

You don't capitalize *devil*, but you do capitalize the names the devil is known by: *Beelzebub, Lucifer, Satan.*

. . .

*S*ports teams are no different than anything else. Common nouns and terms are lowercased, and proper nouns are (capitalized) The only difference may be that because the team names usually include a city or state name, there are many capitalizations.

Still, the rest of the terms remain lowercase. I saw the following headline a few months ago:

- The Women's Soccer Team won the Eastern Region's playoff last night.

That should have been written like this:

- The women's soccer team won the eastern region's playoff last night.

Some general rules to follow:

The sport is (not capitalized)

The words *championship*, *playoff*, *regional*, etc., are not capitalized (unless they are part of a proper noun, such as Gymnastics World Championship).

The roles of team members are not capitalized either. In a report, you wouldn't say "The Coach did this," or "The Team Captain did that," or "The Offensive Coach or Defensive Coach . . ."

All the above terms would be lowercased.

Team names are typically (capitalized) Below are a few examples.

- Boston Red Sox
- New York Yankees

- New York Giants
- San Diego Padres
- Dallas Cowboys
- Pittsburgh Steelers

These are the names of the teams, so the entire name is (capitalized) Even if you refer to them in shortened form, like "I think the Steelers will beat the Cowboys on Sunday," you capitalize both team names.

Card games and board games are capitalized differently. If it's a brand name like Monopoly, Scrabble, or Taboo, the name is obviously (capitalized) But if it is a generic card game, it follows the other rules of capitalization:

- poker
- Texas hold 'em
- canasta
- rummy
- scopa
- blackjack
- Mississippi stud

Personifications

One area of capitalization most of us never come across is personification. You may see it in some writing—poetry more often than any.

Personification is the practice of assigning human qualities to inanimate things or showing humans to represent abstract ideas. If someone is always nice, considerate, and thoughtful, they may be said to be "the personification of kindness"; on the other hand (especially in poetry), you may see phrases such as "the angry red sky."

In the following sentence, *winter* is capitalized because you have given the season human qualities by naming it "Old Man":

- Old Man *Winter* forced him to button his coat tightly.
- *Justice* (*Lady Justice*) always carries her scales and sword.

The reference to Justice dates back to ancient Roman times, when Justice was depicted carrying scales in one hand and a sword in the other. She is now usually seen wearing a blindfold, but that didn't happen until a few hundred years ago.

The scales represent the fairness and equality of justice, the sword the punishment aspect, the blindfold the impartiality of law. In any sense, it is a good example of personification.

Mathematical Formulas, Theorems, and Laws

If a mathematical or scientific law, principle, or theorem contains a proper noun (ordinarily the person it was named after), capitalize that portion of the law:

- Einstein's theory of relativity
- <u>Archimedes' principle</u>
- Fibonacci numbers (or sequence)
- Euclid's theorem
- Marconi's law

And then you have the popular (but specifically named) "laws," which are fully capitalized:

- Murphy's Law
- the Peter Principle
- Occam's Razor
- Asimov's Three Laws of Robotics

Part Eight

ANIMAL BREEDS

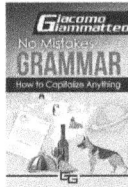

The capitalization of breeds is a touchy subject, especially when referring to dog and cat breeds, although horses and cattle aren't far behind.

The logic on breed capitalization, however, is fairly straightforward. Begin with the rules of *The Chicago Manual of Style* or *Associated Press*, and rationalize the exceptions not explained by those rules—there are always exceptions, and they're seldom explained.

Let's begin with dogs because that is the breed more people are familiar with (considering there are almost one billion dogs across the globe). There are approximately six hundred million cats, more than one billion pigs, and almost one and a half billion cattle.

Let's stray for a moment. People tend to get emotional about this subject, feeling as if we're demeaning their precious dog or cat by not capitalizing the breed name, but it has nothing to do with that.

We're not saying your dog or cat or anything doesn't deserve capitalization; it does. However, it's their name that deserves it, not the breed name. If you named your German shepherd Max, you would capitalize Max just like you'd capitalize the name of your kids or friends.

The breed name is just describing the type of animal it is, in other words, its ancestry, much like the etymology of a word tells its history. Let's look at a few examples that compare dogs to humans.

- Human > boy > Irish > Sean
- Dog > shepherd > German > Max
- Dog > shepherd > Australian > Mollie
- Human > girl > French > Marie

If you say the examples backward, you'll get an idea of how they relate. (When making the statements about the humans, it sounds odd because we don't talk that way.)

- Sean is an Irish boy that's human.
- Max is a German shepherd that's a dog.
- Mollie is an Australian shepherd that's a dog.
- Marie is a French girl that's human.

If you want to look at it another way, substitute the type of dog (category) for *shepherd*, and substitute an occupation for the gender (boy/girl). And switch them around too.

- Sean is an Irish carpenter.
- Sean is a carpenter that's Irish.
- Max is a working dog (category) that's German.
- Max is a German working dog.

- Marie is a French engineer.
- Marie is an engineer that's French.
- Bear is a hunting dog that's English.
- Bear is an English hunting dog.

When you look at it that way, I think you can see the relationship.

Now look at a few other examples.

A "forest-dwelling herdsman from India" describes the indigenous people of India who live in the forests, much like "Anatolian shepherd dog" describes a dog whose ancestry traces back to the Anatolia region of Turkey and who guards livestock.

You wouldn't capitalize "forest-dwelling herdsman" any more than you would "Anatolian shepherd dog," except for the "Anatolian" part. The breed name is simply a descriptor. It's no different than saying, "He's Chinese," "He's Austrian," "He's white," or "He's black."

Note that *Chinese* and *Austrian* are capitalized, while *white* and *black* are not. It's because *Chinese* and *Austrian* are derived from proper nouns, *China* and *Austria*, while *white* and *black* are merely descriptors.

If you were asked to describe one of your friends, you might write, "She's black" or "She's white," but you wouldn't write, "She's Black" or "She's White." The reason is because *white* and *black* are simply telling you what kind of person they are—what color or ethnicity. It's no different than telling a person what kind of dog it is by mentioning that a dog is a shepherd or a working dog.

To get more specific about a person, you might say they are French or Irish, much like you might say a shepherd dog is Australian or a working dog is German.

Seldom do you run across the need to capitalize until you get down to the specifics. For example, there are many types of working dogs: therapy dogs, herding dogs, guard dogs, service dogs, rescue dogs, sled dogs, hunting dogs, police dogs, etc. You don't see any of those types capitalized, but when you look further, you find breeds whose names derive from proper nouns and need capitalization:

- Border collie
- Irish setter
- German shepherd
- Old English sheepdog

This list may hold a few surprises. *Border* is capitalized because the name derives from the Borders region where Scotland and England meet. "Irish setter" and "German shepherd" are self-explanatory, but "Old English sheepdog" is another exception. We'll explain that later.

The rules for animal breeds are similar to the rules for people; you just have to understand them.

One more example, and then we'll move on.

Saying "Max is a shepherd dog from Germany" is the same as saying "Max is a German shepherd dog." You could also say "Skyler is a shepherd dog from Australia" or "Vik is a shepherd dog from Anatolia." The point is that they are all shepherd dogs, and you are simply pointing out their ancestry: one came from Germany, one from Australia, and one from Anatolia. Certain words are capitalized because the names derive from proper nouns: Germany, Australia, and Anatolia.

It's no different than saying "Rose is a white person from Italy" or "Nick is a white person from France" or "Braden is a white person from Romania." Another way of describing these people would be to say "Rose is Italian" or "Nick is French" or "Braden is Romanian." You are describing the people in the same way you described the dogs, by telling their ancestry. And just like you don't capitalize *white* when describing them, you don't capitalize *shepherd* when describing the dogs.

Another way to look at it is to think of shepherd, terrier, hound, etc., as occupations, much like bricklayer, carpenter, plumber. When you look at it that way, saying "German shepherd, Irish wolfhound," and "Yorkshire terrier" is no different than saying "Italian bricklayer, Irish carpenter," or "German plumber."

Moving on to rules

The rules that most of the style guides are in agreement about are the following:

- Capitalize words that derive their name from proper nouns.
- The *Associated Press* rule for animal breeds is to capitalize the part of the name that is derived from a proper noun and lowercase the part of the name derived from a common noun.

Instructions in the *Chicago Manual of Style* aren't as specific as those from AP; instead it points writers to *Merriam-Webster's*.

The problem with suggesting people go to the dictionary is two-fold.

- Many breed names will not be in the dictionary. For example, try looking up "Miniature Australian shepherd" or "Tibetan mastiff."

I couldn't find Miniature Australian shepherd in any of the dictionaries. When I searched for Tibetan mastiff, I found it in *Merriam-Webster's* unabridged version, but when I searched in the collegiate version, I got this:

Tibetan mastiff.

The word you've entered isn't in the Collegiate Dictionary. Click on a spelling suggestion below or try again using the search bar

I decided to try a few more breed names, and I have shown the results below:

Cane Corso

- *Merriam-Webster Collegiate* = (not capitalized)
- *Merriam-Webster Unabridged* = not found.
- *Oxford English Dictionary* = cane corso: (not capitalized)
- *Cambridge Dictionary* = not found
- The Free Dictionary = found in Wikipedia.
- *American Heritage Dictionary = not found.*

See notes about capitalization in the "Dog Breeds" chapter.

The bottom line is that after searching six major dictionaries, I found what I was looking for only twice. Other than the major breeds, the results were similar for most other searches.

The following is a list of how CMOS recommends capitalizing animal breeds. Mind you, they list these examples with no explanation regarding the logic (or the exceptions).

German shorthaired pointer
Hereford
Maine coon or coon cat
Thoroughbred horse (but purebred dog)
Rhode Island Red
boysenberry
rambler rose

— CHICAGO MANUAL OF STYLE

Questions arise immediately. The first three examples are clear, but when we get to *thoroughbred*, I'm left confused. Thoroughbred isn't named after a proper noun. Why is it capitalized? Unfortunately, CMOS offers no explanation, simply a suggestion for readers to consult CMOS's preferred dictionary: *Merriam-Webster's*

We've already seen the inconsistency of *Merriam-Webster's* even among the different versions (unabridged and collegiate). I checked with other dictionaries, and several had the word *thoroughbred* capitalized, but several did not.

When I dug further into the issue, CMOS forums suggested the word was capitalized to keep it from being confused with *purebred*, though I fail to see how a careful analysis of the context wouldn't clarify any sentence (presuming both words were used correctly). The examples I saw were no more confusing than "German shepherd" or "Great Dane."

Let's move on from *thoroughbred* or *Thoroughbred*.

To further add to the confusion, let's look at *dalmatian*. It is recommended as lowercased by CMOS despite the name deriving from Dalmatia, a region of Croatia.

When you check with *Merriam-Webster*, you get the following:

Unabridged: Dal·ma·tian: noun (capitalized)

: a native or inhabitant of Dalmatia

2 or *dalmatian* also *Dalmatian* dog or *dalmatian* dog
: a large dog of a breed supposed to have originated in Dalmatia having a white short-haired coat with black or brown spots varying from dime to half-dollar size, standing from 19 to 23 inches high, and weighing from 35 to 50 pounds — called also coach dog

— MERRIAM-WEBSTER

Collegiate: dal·ma·tian: noun (lowercase)

>: any of a breed of medium-sized dogs having a white short-haired coat with many black or brown spots

— MERRIAM-WEBSTER

I cover both *Dalmatian* and *thoroughbred* in more detail under their respective breeds.

Sometimes, despite what the style guides say—or don't say—common words need to be capitalized to clarify things.

I have my own rule (or guide) regarding capitalization of breed names.

- Any word that precedes a proper noun should be capitalized to avoid confusion.

Not all breed names are confusing, but to keep the rule simple, I feel it's best to be consistent.

A couple of examples follow:

Great Dane

"Great Dane" has to be capitalized to avoid potential confusion, no matter how far-fetched that confusion may be.

If the breed were spelled according to rules laid out by CMOS and AP, it would be "great Dane." However, spelling it that way could lead to confusion. Imagine—no matter how unlikely—a scenario where someone says "She was a great Dane."

In that sentence, we don't know if they are referring to a great Danish person, a great Danish cat, or anything else that is great and Danish. But if we said, "She was a Great Dane," we'd know the person meant a dog of the Great Dane breed.

Old English sheepdog

This breed may provide a more logical reason for capitalizing common words as part of the breed name. The name of the breed is "Old English sheepdog." If we lowercase the Old and write it as "old English sheepdog," it could be misunderstood.

Someone may think you mean an old English sheepdog (meaning any sheepdog of the English variety that is old—a collie, Border collie, corgi, etc.), when in fact you may be referring to an Old English sheepdog puppy.

The same logic regarding clarity holds true for other breed names even if applied differently. Consider this statement:

- "I saw a German shepherd the other day."

Does that imply you saw a German person who had an occupation as a shepherd? Or did you mean to say

- "I saw a German shepherd dog the other day"?

If there is any possibility of confusion regarding the word or words following the breed name, clarify it by using *dog* (or the appropriate breed).

- It was an Australian shepherd dog.
- He had an Old English sheepdog.
- Anatolian shepherd dog
- Australian cattle dog

By the way, you couldn't say "It was an Australian cattle" because *cattle* is used in the plural form only. You could say "There are fifteen cattle in the field," but you can't say "There is one cattle near the fence." (You can say it, but it wouldn't be correct.)

Getting back to German shepherds—usage and clarity aside—the officially recognized name of the breed is "German shepherd dog," although the American Kennel Club and most other dog-breed organizations capitalize all the words in a breed name, so they would list it as "German Shepherd Dog."

Continuing Exceptions to the Rules

Another breed name issue similar to that of "Great Dane" occurs with "Miniature Australian shepherd dog." Without the capitalization of *miniature*, a statement could be interpreted as someone referring to a miniature Australian shepherd dog; in other words, an Australian shepherd dog that is small.

Capitalizing *miniature* signifies it is part of the breed name, thereby making it clear that the reference is to a "Miniature Australian shepherd dog." The same holds true for the "Miniature American shepherd dog."

In fact, when a breed name contains a proper noun, such as American, German, English, etc., I recommend that any words (related to the name) preceding the proper noun be (capitalized) Words that follow it should be lowercased unless they are also proper nouns. An example of the latter would be "Belgian Malinois."

The Belgian Malinois is named after Belgium, and the name Malinois is derived from Malines, the French name for the breed's Flemish city of origin.

Getting back to clarification, we've seen that some breeds need the name *dog* after the initial title, such as the aforementioned German shepherd dog, but most dog-breed names do not need the word *dog* to distinguish them. *Dog* is usually only needed when the word that follows the proper noun could be mistaken for another word—like *shepherd*.

Consider the following:

- Yorkshire terrier
- Irish setter
- Afghan hound

There is no confusion with these breed names, and, as such, the word *dog* is not needed following the breed name. If someone mentions a Yorkshire terrier, I doubt anyone would confuse it with a terrier from Yorkshire (other than meaning a dog).

The second example presents no confusion either. I don't think anyone is going to interpret what you say as an Irish person who is a setter; in other words, someone who sets or places things.

And what else but dog could we mean when we say Afghan hound? Technically, I suppose we could be referring to a person from Afghanistan who is a hound, or someone who chases after others or who relentlessly pursues something; however, it seems beyond far-fetched.

Bottom Line

This is only the tip of the iceberg as far as capitalization issues with breed names. For a complete look at all dog breeds, as well as cat, cattle, donkey, fowl, goat, horse, sheep, and swine, continue reading and check out the chapters dealing with each.

Animals other than domesticated breeds are capitalized in the same manner. The following are examples, but check with your dictionary of choice regarding capitalization.

- Bengal tiger
- California condor
- Andean condor
- Steller's jay
- Siberian tiger
- Komodo dragon

But it would be lowercase in the following examples:

- red-tailed hawk
- bald eagle
- turkey vulture

I've got a set of three rules regarding capitalizing animal breeds. If you follow these rules, you should be able to properly capitalize any breed of animal. Before you resort to the rules, though, check your dictionary of choice to see if the word has an entry. If it doesn't, proceed.

- Capitalize the portion of the name that is derived from a proper noun.
- Capitalize any word (name element) related to the name which precedes the proper noun.
- Do not capitalize words that follow it unless they are also proper nouns.

Chapter Nineteen

CAT BREEDS

*C*at breeds are no different than any other breed. Most rules state that if the breed name contains a proper noun, you capitalize it. If the words following the proper noun are not proper nouns or derived from proper nouns, keep them lowercased.

I have added my own rule: capitalize the word or words preceding the proper noun, regardless of where the name came from.

Abyssinian: (capitalized) Name from Abyssinia, in Ethiopia.

accicat: (not capitalized) This cat was originally named Ocicat due to its resemblance to an ocelot.

Allerca: (capitalized) Named for the company (Allerca) that is said to have created the first hypoallergenic cat.

Aegean cat: (partially capitalized) Named after the Aegean Islands off Greece.

African golden cat: (partially capitalized) From Africa.

African shorthair: (partially capitalized) From Africa.

Afro-chausie: (capitalized) From Africa. Bred from multiple stock, including wild stock, and named by the breeders who designated it *Felis chaus*.

Alaskan snow cat: (partially capitalized) From Alaska.

Albino Siamese: (capitalized) Name derives from Siam. Albino is capitalized because it precedes the name.

Algerian cat: (partially capitalized) Originated in Algeria.

Alpine lynx: (partially capitalized) From the Alps originally.

alpaca cat: (not capitalized)

American blue: (partially capitalized) From America.

American bobtail: (partially capitalized) From America.

American Cornish rex: (partially capitalized) From America but originated in Cornwall, England.

American curl: (partially capitalized) From America.

American forest cat longhair: (partially capitalized) From America.

American keuda: (partially capitalized) From America.

American longhair: (partially capitalized) From America.

American miniature cat: (partially capitalized) From America.

American polydactyl: (partially capitalized) The *polydactyl* portion of the name means it has more than the usual number of toes.

American ringtail: (partially capitalized) From America.

American shorthair: (partially capitalized) From America.

American snughead: (partially capitalized) From America.

American wirehair: (partially capitalized) From America.

Amur Asian leopard cat: (partially capitalized) From Asia.

Andean mountain cat: (partially capitalized) Name from the Andes.

antipodean cat: (not capitalized) *Antipodean* is a term used by those in the Northern Hemisphere that refers to people or things from Australia or New Zealand.

Applehead Siamese: (capitalized) Siamese comes from Siam.

Arabian mau: (partially capitalized) From Arabia.

ashera: (not capitalized) Bred in America but with stock from several breeds.

Asian golden cat: (partially capitalized) From Asia.

Asian semi-longhair: (partially capitalized) From Asia.

Asiatic wildcat: (partially capitalized) From Asia.

Australian mist: (partially capitalized) From Australia.

Australian tiffanie: (partially capitalized) From Australia.

bagral cat: (not capitalized) Breed is from North America.

Bahraini Dilmun cat: (partially capitalized) From Bahrain and the Saudi Arabian region of Dilmun.

Balinese: (capitalized) Breed originated from cross-breeding a Siamese with a cat which derived its name from the island of Bali, hence the name: Balinese.

bambino: (not capitalized) Breed developed in Italy. *Bambino* is an Italian word for *baby* or *child*.

bay cat: (not capitalized) From Borneo.

Bengal: (capitalized) Named from the Bengal region of India. Not to be confused with the Bengal tiger.

Bengal tiger: (partially capitalized) Named from the Bengal region of India.

Birman: (capitalized) The breed gets its name from *Barman*, the French form of Burma, which is where the breed originated.

black-footed cat: (not capitalized) From Africa.

blynx: (not capitalized) Developed in Canada. It is a hybrid offspring of a bobcat and a lynx.

bobcat: (not capitalized) Native to the United States. It is closely related to the lynx.

Bohemian rex cat: (partially capitalized) Name from Bohemia.

Bombay: (capitalized) Name from Bombay, India.

Bornean clouded leopard: (partially capitalized) Name from Borneo.

bramble cat: (not capitalized) U. S. breed.

Brazilian shorthair: (partially capitalized) From Brazil.

Bristol: (capitalized) I believe it was named after Bristol, England.

British longhair: (partially capitalized) From England.

British shorthair: (partially capitalized) From England

Burmese: (capitalized) From Burma.

Burmilla: (capitalized) First part of name derives from Burma.

California spangled cat: (partially capitalized) Bred in California.

Canadian lynx: (partially capitalized) Native to Canada. Similar to the American bobcat.

caracat: (not capitalized) A cross between a wild caracal and an Absynnian.

caracal: (not capitalized) Wild cat in Africa, like a desert lynx.

Celtic shorthair cat: (partially capitalized) Named from the Celts or the Celtic region.

Ceylon cat: (partially capitalized) Name from Ceylon. Bred in India.

Chantilly: (capitalized) Named after Chantilly, France.

Chartreux: (capitalized) Probably named after the Chartreux Mountains of France.

chausie: (not capitalized) Bred in North America and elsewhere. (Named by the breeders—*Felis chaus*).

cheetah: (not capitalized) Large, wild cat native to Africa.

chestnut brown cat: (not capitalized) Originally known as the havana cat, it is now called the chestnut brown cat.

Chinese harlequin: (partially capitalized) Developed in China.

Chinese mountain cat: (partially capitalized) Wild cat found in the mountainous regions of western China.

Chinese white: (partially capitalized) From China.

classicat: (not capitalized) Bred in New Zealand, it resembles an Ocicat.

clouded leopard: (not capitalized) Roams wild in the Himalayan Mountains.

colocolo: (not capitalized) A small wild cat that roams free in South America.

colourpoint: (not capitalized)

colorpoint shorthair: (not capitalized)

Cornish rex: (partially capitalized) Breed originated in Cornwall, England.

cougar: (not capitalized) Roams wild and is native to North America.

Cymric: (capitalized) The name comes from Cymru, the Welsh name for *Wales*.

desert lynx: (not capitalized) A U.S. breed, not to be confused with a wild lynx.

Devon rex: (partially capitalized) From England and name comes from the Devonshire region.

dogla: (not capitalized) Name is an Indian word for a leopard and tiger hybrid.

Don sphinx: (partially capitalized) Russian breed which derives its name from the Don River region.

dossow cat: (not capitalized) A cross between Sphynx and polydactyl cats.

dragon li: (not capitalized) From China

dwarf cats: (not capitalized) Bred in numerous countries, though breeding them is not recommended.

dwelf cat: (not capitalized) Name is a combination of dwarf and elf.

Egyptian mau: (partially capitalized) From Egypt.

elf cat: not capitalized) Like the dwarf cats, the elf cats are bred for their small size, although many countries do not approve.

Eurasian lynx: (partially capitalized) A lynx from Europe and Asia. Roams wild.

Euro-Chaus: (capitalized) A crossbreed of a jungle cat with a European wildcat.

Euro-chausie: (capitalized) Formed by breeding a domestic to the jungle cats of Africa.

European shorthair: (partially capitalized) From Europe.

exotic: (not capitalized) Bred to be a shorthaired version of the Persian cat.

fishing cat: (not capitalized) Medium-sized wild cat of Asia.

flat-headed cat: (not capitalized) Small wild cat near

Thailand, Borneo, and Sumatra.

foldex cat: (not capitalized) Developed in Québec, Canada.

Geoffroy's cat: (partially capitalized) Small wild cat of central and southern South America. It got its name from Étienne Geoffroy Saint-Hilaire, a French naturalist.

German rex: (partially capitalized) From Germany. (*rex* is Latin for king.)

havana brown: (not capitalized) Crossbreed between Siamese and a black cat. Now known as the chestnut brown breed. The name has nothing to do with the city of Havana; instead, it was named for the deep brown coloring which is said to resemble the coloring of a Havana cigar.

Hemingway curl: (partially capitalized) Named after the writer, Ernest Hemingway, this cat is a polydactyl, meaning it has more toes than usual, and the breed carries the gene for that.

highlander: (not capitalized) A cross between the desert lynx and the jungle curl.

Himalayan: (capitalized) From the United States and other countries. Got its name from the color of animals from the Himalayan Mountains.

Iberian lynx: (partially capitalized) Wild cat native to the Iberian Peninsula.

Iriomote cat: (partially capitalized) This breed is a subspecies of the *leopard cat* and it from the island of Iriomote, in Japan.

jaglion: (not capitalized) A *jaglion* is a cross between a male jaguar and a lioness. This only happens in captivity.

jagupard: (not capitalized) Much the same as above, the *jagupard* is a cross between a male jaguar and a leopardess. (sometimes called a *jagulep*).

jaguar: (not capitalized) A wild cat that is native to South and North America, predominantly in the heavily forested areas.

jaguarundi: (not capitalized) A small, wild cat that is native to the Americas. It ranges as far north as southern Texas.

jaguarundi curl: (not capitalized) See above.

Japanese bobtail: (partially capitalized) From Japan.

Javanese: (capitalized) From the island of Java.

jungle cat: (not capitalized) A medium-sized cat native to the Middle East and Southeast Asia as far as China.

jungle-curl: (not capitalized) A mix between an American curl and a jungle cat.

jungle lynx: (not capitalized) A cross between the bobcat and the wild jungle cat.

Kanaani cat: (partially capitalized) First bred in Jerusalem, the *Kanaani* got its name from the Biblical *Caananite*. It closely resembles its spotted African wildcat ancestors.

kinkalow: (not capitalized) First bred in the 1990s in the United States.

kodkod: (not capitalized) The *kodkod* is the smallest wildcat and is native to central and southern Chile.

Korat: (capitalized) From the Korat province in Thailand.

Kurilian bobtail: (partially capitalized) Found on the Kuril archipelago in Russia.

lambkin: (not capitalized) A breed developed from several other breeds, including the *bambino* and *minskin*.

laPerm: (not capitalized) Developed via a mutation in the state of Oregon, in the United States.

leguar: (not capitalized) A cross between a male leopard and a female jaguar.

leopard: (not capitalized) Wild cat native to Africa.

leopard cat: (not capitalized) A small, wild cat native to sourthern Asia.

leopon: (not capitalized) A cross between a male leopard and a lioness.

li hua mau: (not capitalized) Also known as the *dragon li*. It was developed in China.

liger: (not capitalized) Cross between a male lion and a female tiger.

liguar: (not capitalized) Cross between a male lion and a female jaguar.

lion: (not capitalized) Large wild cat native to Africa.

lynx: (not capitalized) Wild cat that is similar to the American bobcat. Native to Canada, the Iberian Peninsula, Asia, and elsewhere.

lynxcat: (not capitalized) Cross between a bobcat and a lynx

machbagral: (not capitalized) Created by crossing the Asian fishing cat with a tabby.

mandalan jaguar: (not capitalized) The only information I could find on this was that it was a proposed name for a cross between a jaguarandi and a domestic cat.

margay: (not capitalized) Small, wild cat native to Central and South America.

marbled cat: (not capitalized) A small, wild cat native to the Himalayas and Southeast Asia.

marlot: (not capitalized) A cross between a *margay* and an ocelot.

Maine coon: (partially capitalized) From Maine. Many stories mention ways in which the *coon* portion got its name, including a ship's captain, a cabin boy, and others, however, none can be verified enough to consider it a capitalized word.

Maltese cat: (not capitalized) A *Maltese* is any cat whose fur is either completely, or primarily, gray or blue and is of indeterminate breed. Supposedly there are many such cats on the island of Malta, hence the naming.

Manx: (capitalized) It originated on the Isle of Man where it got its name. (it used to be *manks*). The Manx is easily identified by the naturally occurring mutation that shortens the tail. Some of the cats appear to have no tail, while others appear to have a bobtail.

Mekong bobtail cat: (partially capitalized) Originated in the Mekong Delta region of Thailand and Southeast Asia.

miniature: (not capitalized)

minskin: (not capitalized) A cross between *munchin* and *sphinx* cats.

Modern Siamese: (capitalized)

moggy: (not capitalized) British slang name for a *mongrel cat.*

Munchkin: (capitalized) The Munchkin is a smaller cat with shortened legs (originally through mutation). It was given its name from "*The Wizard of Oz Munchkins,*" the little people who helped Dorothy. Aside from that, there is also some speculation that the name *Munchkin* is derived somehow from *Munich*.

Napoleon: (capitalized) A cross between the Munchkin and the Persian, this breed's name derives from the diminutive Emperor.

nebelung: (not capitalized) The name means "creature of the mist" in German.

Norwegian forest cat: (partially capitalized) From Norway.

ocelot: (not capitalized) Wild cat native to the Americas.

ocicat: (not capitalized) A cross between the Abyssinian,

Siamese, and American Shorthair.

odd-eyed cat: (not capitalized)

ojos azules: (not capitalized) Breed originated in the Southwestern United States. Its name derives from Spanish meaning *"blue eyes."*

oncilla: (not capitalized) Small, wild cat ranging from Brazil to Central America.

Oregon rex cat: (partially capitalized) From Oregon.

Oriental longhair: (partially capitalized) Name comes from *Orient*.

Oriental shorthair: (partially capitalized) Name comes from *Orient*.

Pallas's cat: (partially capitalized) A small, wild cat in central Asia. Name came from scientist Peter Simon Pallas.

Pampas cat: (partially capitalized) A small, wild cat native to South America and named after the Pampas region.

Pantanal cat: (partially capitalized) A small, wild cat native to South America. It is named after the Pantanal wetlands.

Persian: (capitalized) Name derives from Persia.

Peterbald: (capitalized) Breed originated in Russia, in St. Petersburgh.

pixie-bob: (not capitalized)

Punjabi: (capitalized) Named after the Indian region of Punjab.

pumapard: (not capitalized) A cross between a male puma and a female leopard.

polydactyl cat: (not capitalized) A polydactyl cat is simply one that has more than the usual number of toes.

ragdoll: (not capitalized) The name comes from the breed's tendency to go limp, *like a ragdoll* when picked up.

ragamuffin: (not capitalized) A breed that is a variant of the *ragdoll*.

Russian: (capitalized) From Russia.

Russian blue: (partially capitalized) From Russia.

rusty-spotted cat: (not capitalized)

sand cat: (not capitalized) The only cat known to live mostly in deserts. It is found in North Africa, the Middle East, and Central Asia.

Scottie-chausie: (partially capitalized) From Scotland.

Scottish fold: (partially capitalized) From Scotland.

safari: (not capitalized) The safari breed was developed using stock from the Geoffrey breed.

savannah: (not capitalized) A cross between a serval and a domestic cat.

selkirk rex: (not capitalized) The breed is different from other rex breeds in that the hair is of normal length and none of it is missing. It originated in Montana during the 1980s.

Serengeti: (capitalized) A breed named after the region in Africa, and developed using wild cat and domestic stock.

serval: (not capitalized) Found wild cat native to Africa.

servical: (not capitalized) A cross between the caraval and serval breeds.

Seychellois: (capitalized) Name from the Seychelles Islands.

Shorthaired Birman: (capitalized) Name derives from *Birmanie*, the French form of Burma.

Siamese: (capitalized) From Siam.

Siberian: (capitalized) Name from Siberia.

Singapura: (capitalized) Name from Singapore.

skookum: (not capitalized) Name comes from an Indian word originating in the Pacific Northwest.

snow leopard: (not capitalized) A wild cat native to the mountain ranges of central and south Asia.

snowshoe: (not capitalized)

Sokoke: (capitalized) A breed of domestic cat. It is named after the Arabuko Sokoke National Forest.

Somali: (capitalized) Named after Somalia.

sphynx: (not capitalized)

squitten: (not capitalized)

tabby cat: (not capitalized) Domestic cat with distinctive markings.

teacup cats: (not capitalized)

templecat: (not capitalized)

Thai: (capitalized) Named after Thailand.

tiffany: (not capitalized)

tiger: (not capitalized) Largest of the wild cats.

Tonkinese: (capitalized) Name from the Tonkin people of North Vietnam.

tortoiseshell cat: (not capitalized)

Traditional Siamese: (capitalized) Name from Siam.

Turkish Angora: (capitalized) From Turkey and from the Ankara region of Turkey.

Turkish van: (partially capitalized) Bred in England using several breeds from Turkey.

Ukrainian levkoy: (partially capitalized) The breed is almost hairless with inner-folding ears.

Urals rex: (partially capitalized) From Russia, near the Ural Mountains.

Ussuri: (capitalized) Named after the Ussuri RIver in Russia and China.

viverral cat: (not capitalized) A cross between the fishing cat and the Bengal.

York cat: (partially capitalized) The breed was established in the United States and named after New York, where it was originally bred.

Chapter Twenty

CATTLE BREEDS

I need to give thanks to the Oklahoma State University for providing many of these breed names. I also need to recognize Wikipedia as a provider of information regarding the origin of some of the names.

In keeping with policy and to remain consistent across all breeds, I have continued to capitalize the name elements that precede a proper noun. Not all words would cause confusion, but I felt it better to keep things the same.

Because we'll be discussing many domesticated livestock breeds, we're going to run across the word *landrace* a lot. *Landrace* simply refers to an animal breed that has been improved by traditional agricultural methods.

Now on to the list.

Africander cattle: (partially capitalized) Named after South Africa.

akaushi: (not capitalized) From Japan.

Alberes cattle: (partially capitalized) The Alberes are a semi-feral breed found in the Albères Mountains and eastern Pyrenees of France and Spain.

Alentejana cattle: (partially capitalized) Breed is from the region of Alentejo, Portugal.

allmogekor cattle: (not capitalized) The Swedish name "allmogekor" refers to peasant cattle.

American: (capitalized) Breed from America.

American braford cattle: (partially capitalized) Bred in both America and Australia.

American breed cattle: (partially capitalized) Bred in America.

American white park cattle: (partially capitalized) Bred in America.

amerifax cattle: (not capitalized) Bred in America.

amrit mahal cattle: (not capitalized) "Amrit mahal" means "department of milk" in Pakistani where the breed originated.

Anatolian black cattle: (partially capitalized) From the Anatolian region of Turkey.

Andalusian black cattle: (partially capitalized) From the Andalusia region of Spain.

Andalusian grey cattle: (partially capitalized) From the Andalusia region of Spain.

Angein cattle: (partially capitalized) From the northern part of Germany, the Angein region near the Danish border.

Angus cattle: (partially capitalized) From the county of Angus in northern Scotland.

Ankole cattle: (partially capitalized) From the Ankole region of Uganda.

Ankole-Watusi cattle: (partially capitalized) From the Ankole region of Uganda and the Watuse people.

Argentine criollo cattle: (partially capitalized) From Argentina.

Asturian mountain cattle: (partially capitalized) From the Asturias mountain region of Spain.

Asturian valley cattle: (partially capitalized) From the Asturias Valley of Spain, not far from the mountains.

Aubrac cattle: (partially capitalized) From the l'Aubrac region of France.

Aulie-Ata cattle: (partially capitalized) From the Aulie-Ata region of Kirgizia.

Australian braford cattle: (partially capitalized) Breed developed in the United States and Australia.

Australian Friesian Sahiwal cattle: (partially capitalized) Bred using three prime breeds, all three words derive from regions and therefore need to be (capitalized)

Australian lowline cattle: (partially capitalized) From Australia.

Australian milking zebu cattle: (partially capitalized) From Australia.

Ayrshire cattle: (partially capitalized) From the county of Ayr in Scotland.

Ayrshire cattle: (partially capitalized) From the county of Ayr in Scotland.

Ayrshire cattle Registries: (partially capitalized) From the county of Ayr in Scotland.

Azaouak: (capitalized) From the Azoauak Basin in NW Niger, Africa.

Bachaur cattle: (partially capitalized) Breed comes from the Bachaur and Koilpur regions of India.

baladi cattle: (not capitalized) Baladi means "of the country" in Egyptian. The breed began in the Middle East, possibly Syria, Israel, Jordon, etc.

Baltata Romaneasca cattle: (partially capitalized) Also known as the Romanian spotted cattle. We'll stand by policy and keep *baltata* capitalized since it precedes the proper noun; otherwise it could be called any Romanian cattle with spots, instead of a "Spotted Romanian cattle."

Barka cattle: (partially capitalized) Likely named after the Barka River or the Barka province of Eritrea in Ethiopia.

Barzona cattle: (partially capitalized) Most likely the name derived from the breed developer, F. N. Bard combined with the state where he developed it—Arizona. Since both would be proper nouns and require capitalization, I feel the breed name should be (capitalized)

Bazadais cattle: (partially capitalized) The exact naming of this breed is unknown, but it may be assumed to have come from the Bazas region of France.

Béarnais cattle: (partially capitalized) Breed originates in the area of the traditional province of Béarn, in France. It takes its name from the region as well as the Béarnais people, much like the sauce did.

beefalo cattle: (not capitalized) The beefalo is simply a cross between bison and cattle of any breed.

beefmaker cattle: (not capitalized)

beefmaster cattle: (not capitalized) Bred in Texas.

Belarus red cattle: (partially capitalized) Bred in the Belarus region of Russia, the breed contains the bloodlines of numerous *reds*, such as German Red , Polish Red, and Danish Red, among others.

Belgian blue cattle: (partially capitalized) Originated in Belgium.

Belgian red cattle: (partially capitalized) Originated in Belgium.

Belmont adaptaur cattle: (partially capitalized) The

breed was established on the Belmont Research Station near Rockhampton, Queensland.

Belmont red cattle: (partially capitalized) The breed was also established on the Belmont Research Station near Rockhampton, Queensland.

Belted Galloway cattle: (partially capitalized) Originated in the Galloway region of Scotland. The belted part of the name speaks to the coloring, a white stripe that runs between black, however, in keeping with policy, it is capitalized because it precedes the proper noun.

Bengali cattle: (partially capitalized) Originated in Benal, India and Bangladesh.

berrendas cattle: (not capitalized) From Spain. Word comes from Spanish similar to mult-colored or mottled.

Bhagnari cattle: (partially capitalized) Come from the Bhag territory in north of district of Baluchistan.

Blacksided Trondheim and Norland cattle: (partially capitalized) Breed originated in Norway near the Trondelag and Nordland counties.

Blanca Cacereña cattle: (partially capitalized) Also known as White Cáceres, the breed originated in the Cáceres region of Spain.

blanco orejinegro cattle: (not capitalized) The name means "white black-eared." From Columbia, South America.

Blonde d'Aquitaine cattle: (partially capitalized) Name derives from the Aquitaine region of France.

Boran cattle: (partially capitalized) Name comes from the Borana people of Ethiopia.

Bordelais cattle: (partially capitalized) Name comes from the Bordeaux region of France, from which many things took their name: Bordeaux wine, Bordelais sauce, the

Bordeleis grape, and many more. (Note the different spellings.)

Brahman cattle: (partially capitalized) Name may come from Brahma, the Hindu deity.

Brahmousin cattle: (partially capitalized) The name came from a cross between Brahman and Limousin, both of which are proper nouns, as Brahman came from Brahma, and Limousin came from the region of France with the same name.

Brangus cattle: (partially capitalized) Name comes from crossing Angus cattle with Brahman cattle, and since both derive from proper nouns, this should be capitalized also.

braunvieh cattle: (not capitalized) Braunvieh is a German word meaning "brown cattle."

British white cattle: (partially capitalized) From England.

Brown Swiss cattle: (partially capitalized) From Switzerland.

bua cattle: (not capitalized) From Bosnia.

cachena cattle: (not capitalized) From Spain.

Canadian highland cattle: (partially capitalized) From Canada.

Canadienne cattle: (partially capitalized) From Canada.

Canary Island cattle: (partially capitalized) From the Canary Islands.

canchim cattle: (not capitalized) From Brazil

Carinthian blond cattle: (partially capitalized) Nmae derives from the Carinthia region of Austria.

Caucasian cattle: (partially capitalized) Named after the Caucusus Mountain region.

channi cattle: (not capitalized) Breed comes from India and Pakistan.

Charbray cattle: (partially capitalized) Name derives from a cross between the Brahman and the Charolais, which derives its name from the Charolles region of France.

Charolais cattle: (partially capitalized) The Charolais derives its name from the Charolles region of France.

Chianina cattle: (partially capitalized) The breed originated in the Chiana Valley in Tuscany, Italy. It is one of the oldest breeds known.

chinampo cattle: (not capitalized) The breed name is a Mexican term that has to do with the area the cattle are raised in.

Chinese black-and-white cattle: (partially capitalized) From China.

Chinese Mongolian cattle: (partially capitalized) From China and Mongolia.

Chinese Xinjiang brown cattle: (partially capitalized) Cattle from the Xinjiang region of China.

Cholistani cattle: (partially capitalized) Got its name from the Cholistan desert in Pakistan.

corriente cattle: (not capitalized) From South America. The name comes from the Mexican word for "small cattle."

costeño con cuernos cattle: (not capitalized) Name comes from Spanish meaning "coast dweller with horns."

Dajal cattle: (partially capitalized) Cattle are from the Dajal region of Pakistan.

Damascus cattle: (partially capitalized) Name probably derives from Damascus despite the breed being found in Turkey as well as Syria.

Damietta cattle: (partially capitalized) Named after the Damietta region.

Dangi cattle: (partially capitalized) Takes its name from the Dangs region of India.

Danish Jersey cattle: (partially capitalized) Danish and Jersey both derive from proper names, so they are (capitalized)

Danish red cattle: (partially capitalized) Danish is (capitalized)

deoni cattle: (not capitalized) Got its name from the Indian word meaning "of the hills."

Devon cattle: (partially capitalized) From the Devon region of England.

Dexter cattle: (partially capitalized) Some claim the name derives from a Mr. Dexter who began the breed in Ireland.

Dhanni cattle: (partially capitalized) Named after a region of Pakistan.

dølafe cattle: (not capitalized) From Norway.

droughtmaster cattle: (not capitalized) From Australia. The breed was begun to adapt to and survive the rugged Australian climate, hence its name.

Dulong cattle: (partially capitalized) Comes from the region around Dulong county where it gets its name. From China.

Dutch belted (Lakenvelder) cattle: (partially capitalized) Found in the Netherlands. The name *Lakenvelder* is thought to come from the village of Lakerveld,

Dutch friesian cattle: (partially capitalized) From the Netherlands.

East Anatolian red cattle: (partially capitalized) From Turkey and gets the name from Anatolia.

Enderby Island cattle: (partially capitalized) Name comes from Enderby Island off New Zealand's coast.

English longhorn cattle: (partially capitalized) From England.

Estonian red cattle: (partially capitalized) From Estonia.

Evolène: (capitalized) From Switzerland, and the name likely derives from the village of Evolène.

fighting cattle: (not capitalized) Bred in Spain, Portugal, France, and Latin America. Also known as the fighting bull.

Finnish cattle: (partially capitalized) From Finland.

fjall cattle: (not capitalized) From Sweden.

Florida cracker cattle: (partially capitalized) Similar to the Texas longhorn, this breed comes from Florida as the name suggests.

Galician blond cattle: (partially capitalized) From Galicia in Spain.

Galloway cattle: (partially capitalized) Name derives from the Galloway region and the Gaul people. Breed is in England.

gaolao cattle: (not capitalized) From India.

Gascon cattle: (partially capitalized) From the Gascony region of France.

gelbvieh cattle: (not capitalized) *Gelbvieh* is German for "yellow cattle."

gelbray: (not capitalized) Breed from the United States. It is a result of mixing gelbvieh, red angus and Brahman genetics.

German Angus moiled cattle: (partially capitalized) *Angus* is a proper noun and they come from Germany.

German red pied cattle: (partially capitalized) From Germany.

Gir cattle: (partially capitalized) Name probably comes from the Gir National Forest in India. Possibly from the Gir province in Iran but either way, it would be (capitalized)

Glan cattle: (partially capitalized) Name comes from the

Glan River in Germany, or possibly Glan Lake in nearby Sweitzerland.

Gloucester cattle: (partially capitalized) Name comes from Gloucester, England.

gobra: (not capitalized) Breed comes from Senegal, in Africa.

Greek shorthorn cattle: (partially capitalized) Breed comes from Greece.

Greek steppe cattle: (partially capitalized) Breed comes from Greece.

Groningen cattle: (partially capitalized) Gronings is a city in the Netherlands where the cattle are from.

Guernsey cattle: (partially capitalized) From the Isle of Guernsey off England.

Guzerat cattle: (partially capitalized) *Gujarat* is a region of western India and is another way of spelling *Guzerat*.

hallikar cattle: (not capitalized) From India.

Hariana cattle: (partially capitalized) Named after the Indian state of Haryana in the north.

harton cattle: (not capitalized) From Columbia, brought by the Spanish hundreds of years ago.

Hays converter cattle: (partially capitalized) Named after Senator Hays of Canada.

Hereford cattle: (partially capitalized) Named after Herefordshire, England.

Herens cattle: (partially capitalized) Named after the Herens region of Switzerland.

Highland cattle: (partially capitalized) Named after the Scottish Highlands.

Hinterwald cattle: (partially capitalized) Name comes from Hinterwald, Germany.

Holando-Argentino cattle: (partially capitalized) The

breed was introduced into Argentina from Holland, hence the name.

Holstein cattle: (partially capitalized) Named for the Holstein region in Germany.

horro cattle: (not capitalized) From Ethiopia.

Hungarian grey cattle: (partially capitalized) From Hungary.

Icelandic cattle: (partially capitalized) From Iceland.

illawarra cattle: (not capitalized) The breed got its name from the word used by Australian aborigines to describe the land around Sydney, Australia.

Indo-Brazilian cattle: (partially capitalized) The breed is from Brazil, but used stock from India.

Irish moiled cattle: (partially capitalized) From Ireland.

Israeli Holstein cattle: (partially capitalized) From Israel, using imported Holstein bulls.

Israeli red cattle: (partially capitalized) From Israel.

Istoben cattle: (partially capitalized) From Russia and named after the village of Istoben.

Jamaica black cattle: (partially capitalized) From Jamaica.

Jamaica hope cattle: (partially capitalized) From Jamaica.

Jamaica red cattle: (partially capitalized) From Jamaica.

Jaulan cattle: (partially capitalized) Probably named after the Jaulan district in Syria.

Jersey cattle: (partially capitalized) Named after the Isle of Jersey off the coast of England.

Kangayam cattle: (partially capitalized) Named after the Kangayam district in India.

Kankrej cattle: (partially capitalized) Named after the Kankrej district in India.

Karan Fries cattle: (partially capitalized) Breed was developed in India using the Friesian and Tharparkar cattle.

Karan Swiss cattle: (partially capitalized) From India, using a Swiss breed.

Kazakh cattle: (partially capitalized) Got its name from Kazakhstan.

Kenwariya cattle: (partially capitalized) Name comes from the River Ken in India.

Kerry cattle: (partially capitalized) From the Kerry region of Ireland.

Kherigarh cattle: (partially capitalized) Breed originated in the Kheri district of India.

khillari cattle: (not capitalized) *Khillar* means "a herd of cattle" in India.

Kholmogory cattle: (partially capitalized) From the Kholmogory region of Russia.

Kilis cattle: (partially capitalized) Named after a city in Turkey.

Krishna Valley cattle: (partially capitalized) Named after the Krishna Valley in India.

Kurdi black cattle: (partially capitalized) Named after the Kurds of Kurdistan.

Kuri cattle: (partially capitalized) Named after the Kuri people of Africa.

Latvian brown cattle: (partially capitalized) From Latvia.

Limousin cattle: (partially capitalized) Named after the Limousin region of France.

Limpurger cattle: (partially capitalized) From the Limpurg region of Germany.

Lincoln red cattle: (partially capitalized) Named after

Lincolnshire in England where it was imported into Australia from.

Lithuanian red cattle: (partially capitalized) Name from Lithuania.

Lohani cattle: (partially capitalized) From the Loralai district in Pakistan.

Lourdais cattle: (partially capitalized) Named for the town of Lourdes in France.

Luing cattle: (partially capitalized) Developed on the Isle of Luing off the coast of Scotland.

Madagascar zebu cattle: (partially capitalized) From Madagascar.

Maine-Anjou cattle: (partially capitalized) Developed in Maine with imported stock from France.

Malvi cattle: (partially capitalized) Bred mostly in the Malwa section of Madhyabharat State, in India.

Mandalong cattle: (partially capitalized) Developed at Mandalong Park in Australia.

Marchigiana cattle: (partially capitalized) Got its name from the Marche region of Italy.

Maremmana cattle: (partially capitalized) From the Maremma region of Italy.

Masai cattle: (partially capitalized) From the Massai people of Africa.

Mashona cattle: (partially capitalized) Name comes from the Shona people of Zimbabwe, Africa.

Maure cattle: (partially capitalized) From Mauritania, Africa.

Mazandarani cattle: (partially capitalized) From the Mazandaran province of Iran.

Meuse-Rhine-Yssel cattle: (partially capitalized) The

breed got its name from the area in the Netherlands where three rivers meet: the Meuse, Rhine, and Issel.

Mewati cattle: (partially capitalized) From the Mewat region of India.

Milking Devon cattle: (partially capitalized) Breed is associated with the United States, but it got its name from the Devon region in England.

milking shorthorn cattle: (not capitalized) From England.

modicana cattle: (not capitalized) From Sicily.

Mongolian: (capitalized) Originated in Mongolia.

Montbéliard cattle: (partially capitalized) Named after Montbéllard, a city in western France.

morucha cattle: (not capitalized) Moroucha describes "someone or something with both light and dark hair." The breed is from Spain.

Murboden cattle: (partially capitalized) Named after the Murboden region of Austria. The breed is found in Austria and Slovenia.

Murray grey cattle: (partially capitalized) Named after the Murray River in Australia.

muturu—West African dwarf shorthorn: (partially capitalized) From West Africa. If referred to as *muter*, it isn't capitalized, but if *West African dwarf* is used, capitalization is as stated above.

Nagori cattle: (partially capitalized) Originated in the Nagaur region of India.

Nanyang cattle: (partially capitalized) From the Nanyang region of China.

Nelore cattle: (partially capitalized) Brought to Brazil from India, they got their name from the Nellore region of India.

Nimari cattle: (partially capitalized) From the Nimar region of India.

Normande cattle: (partially capitalized) From Normandy, France.

Norwegian red cattle: (partially capitalized) From Norway.

Ongole cattle: (partially capitalized) From the Ongole region of India.

oropa cattle: (not capitalized) From Italy.

Ovambo cattle: (partially capitalized) Name comes from the Ovambo people of Namibia.

Parthenais cattle: (partially capitalized) Name comes from the town of Parthenay, in France.

Philippine native cattle: (partially capitalized) From the Philippines.

Piedmontese cattle: (partially capitalized) Name derived from the Piemonte region of Italy.

Pinzgauer cattle: (partially capitalized) Named after Pinzgau region of Austria.

Polish red cattle: (partially capitalized) From Poland.

Polled Hereford: (capitalized) Hereford comes from Herefordshire.

Ponwar cattle: (partially capitalized) From the Ponwar district in India.

qinchuan cattle: (not capitalized) From China.

Rath cattle: (partially capitalized) From Rajasthan region of India.

Rathi cattle: (partially capitalized) From Rajasthan region of India.

Red Angus cattle: (partially capitalized) From Angus, Scotland.

Red Brangus cattle: (partially capitalized) From Angus,

Scotland and from the Brahman breed.

Red Fulani or Mbororo: (capitalized) Named after the Fulani and/or Bororo people of Nigeria.

Red Pied Friesian cattle: (partially capitalized) Named after Frisia in Germany.

red poll cattle: (not capitalized) England.

Red Sindhi cattle: (partially capitalized) From the Pakistani state of Sind.

Reggiana cattle: (partially capitalized) Found in the Reggio Emilia region of Italy.

retinta cattle: (not capitalized) From Spain.

Rojhan cattle: (partially capitalized) From the Rojhan region of Pakistan.

Romosinuano cattle: (partially capitalized) Breed is from Columbia, and the name comes from the Sinú Valley of northern Columbia. It means "polled sinu."

Russian black pied cattle: (partially capitalized) From Russia.

Sahiwal cattle: (partially capitalized) Name comes from Sahiwal, a city in Pakistan.

Salers cattle: (partially capitalized) Originated in the Sa'lair region of France.

salorn cattle: (not capitalized) From Texas.

San Martinero cattle: (partially capitalized) Named after the San Martîn province. Breed is from Columbia.

Sanhe cattle: (partially capitalized) From Mongolia. Named for the Sanhe district.

Santa Cruz cattle: (partially capitalized) Breed originated in Texas (King Ranch).

Santa Gertrudis cattle: (partially capitalized) Originally from Spain and named after Saint Gertrude.

Sarabi cattle: (partially capitalized) Name probably

came from Sarab county in northern Iran.

senepol cattle: (not capitalized) From St. Croix.

Shetland cattle: (partially capitalized) Name from the Shetland Islands off Scotland.

shorthorn cattle: (not capitalized) From England.

Siboney cattle: (partially capitalized) Possibly named for Siboney, a town in Cuba, where the breed comes from.

simbrah cattle: (not capitalized) From Texas.

Simmental cattle: (partially capitalized) Named for the Simmental Valley of Switzerland.

siri cattle: (not capitalized) India.

Slovenian cika cattle: (partially capitalized) From Slovenia.

South Devon cattle: (partially capitalized) Named after the Devon region of England.

Sudanese Fulani: (capitalized) From Sudan and the Fulani people of that region.

Sussex cattle: (partially capitalized) From the Sussex region of England.

Swedish Friesian cattle: (partially capitalized) Breed is from Sweden and mixed with stock from Frisia, a region in Germany.

Swedish red polled cattle: (partially capitalized) From Sweden.

Swedish red-and-white cattle: (partially capitalized) From Sweden.

Tarentaise cattle: (partially capitalized) Name comes from the Tarentaise Valley in the French Alpine mountains.

Telemark cattle: (partially capitalized) Region in Norway.

Texas longhorn cattle: (partially capitalized) Breed is from Texas.

Texon cattle: (partially capitalized) Name derives from crossbreeding the Texas longhorn and the Devon.

Tharparkar cattle: (partially capitalized) From the Tharparkar district in India.

Tswana cattle: (partially capitalized) Name comes from the Tswana people of Botswana.

Turkish grey steppe cattle: (partially capitalized) From Turkey's steppes.

Ukrainian beef cattle: (partially capitalized) From the Ukraine.

Ukrainian grey cattle: (partially capitalized) From the Ukraine.

Ukrainian whitehead cattle: (partially capitalized) From the Ukraine.

umblachery cattle: (not capitalized)

Ural black pied cattle: (partially capitalized) Name from the Ural Mountains in Russia.

Vestland fjord cattle: (partially capitalized) Name comes from the Vestland region of Norway.

Vestland red polled cattle: (partially capitalized) Name comes from the Vestland region of Norway.

Vosges cattle: (partially capitalized) Originally from the Vosges Mountain region of Germany.

waygu cattle: (not capitalized) *Wagyu* means "Japanese style cattle."

Welsh black cattle: (partially capitalized) From Wales.

white park cattle: (not capitalized) Imported from England into Canada and the United States.

Yanbian cattle: (partially capitalized) Named after a region in China.

I hope this answers any questions you have regarding capitalizing cattle breeds. If I missed any, let me know.

Chapter Twenty-One

DOG BREEDS

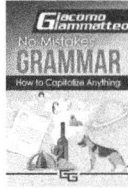

*E*veryone knows several dog breeds, or at least the breed of dog you own or that of a neighbor, but the American Kennel Club (AKC) lists 175 breeds, and that represents only the breeds they approve of; there are many more.

The AKC capitalizes all dog breeds, but that's not recommended according to CMOS and AP, the two primary style guides. Those guides suggest capitalizing only the portion of the breed name that derives from a proper noun, such as *German* in German shepherd dog.

The problem with the rules as stated by both style guides is they don't explain the exceptions—and there are exceptions. You'll see a few of them as we go through the list.

At the beginning of the "Animal Breeds" section, we discussed some of the logic in assigning upper- or lowercase letters to breed names; now we'll look at the specifics on each name.

The complete list of dog breeds (from the AKC):

affenpinscher: (not capitalized) The name is German for "ape (or monkey) terrier."

Afghan hound: (partially capitalized) Named after Afghanistan.

Airedale terrier: (partially capitalized) From England and named after the River Aire. A *dale* is a synonym for valley, so Airedale literally means "valley of Aire."

Akita: (capitalized) Originated in the Akita section of Honshu, the northernmost province of Japan.

Alaskan Malamute: (capitalized) From Alaska and Malemiut, a people who inhabited Alaska.

American English coonhound: (partially capitalized) From America and England.

American Eskimo dog: (partially capitalized) From America and the Eskimo people of Alaska.

American foxhound: (partially capitalized) From America. This breed was used for hunting foxes.

American Staffordshire terrier: (partially capitalized) Name comes from America and the Staffordshire region of England.

American water spaniel: (partially capitalized) Name comes from America.

Anatolian shepherd dog: (partially capitalized) Name comes from the Anatolia region in Turkey.

Australian cattle dog: (partially capitalized) Name comes from Australia. Dog is used in herding of livestock.

Australian shepherd: (partially capitalized) Name comes from Australia.

Australian terrier: (partially capitalized) Name comes from Australia.

basenji: (not capitalized) Name comes from the language of the Congo, where the name means "villager dogs."

basset hound: (not capitalized) From France, where it got its name from the French words for "rather low" referring to the noise it makes. Basset hounds are said to have a sense of smell second to only the bloodhounds.

beagle: (not capitalized) *Beagle* comes from the word *beagling* which means "to hunt hares and rabbits with hounds," which is what beagles are used for.

bearded collie: (not capitalized) Bred in Scotland using Polish sheepdogs and local Scottish dogs. The name is possibly derived from *coaly*, meaning "coal black."

Beauceron: (capitalized) From the Beuce region of France. It is often referred to as the Berger de Beuce, which means "sheepdog from Beuce."

Bedlington terrier: (partially capitalized) Named after the town of Bedlington, England where the breed originated.

Belgian Malinois: (capitalized) Named after Belgium and *Malinois*, which is derived from *Malines*, the French name for the breed's Flemish city of origin: Mechelen.

Belgian sheepdog: (capitalized) From Belgium and the Tevuren region of Belgium.

Belgian Tervuren: (partially capitalized) From Belgium.

Bernese mountain dog: (partially capitalized) The name derives from the city of Bern and the nearby Bernese Mountains. A note on the capitalization. *Mountain* is not capitalized because the name is using mountain as an adjective to describe dog. It is named after the Bernese *mountains* (plural), not a single mountain.

bichon frise: (not capitalized) The breed name is French for "curly lap dog."

Black Russian terrier: (partially capitalized) From Russia.

black and tan coonhound: (not capitalized)

bloodhound: (not capitalized)

Blue Lacy: (capitalized) The Lacy dog was named after the Lacy brothers (Frank, George, Ewin, and Harry Lacy) who moved from Kentucky to Texas in 1858 and settled near San Antonio. According to the Lacy family, the dog was a mixture of English shepherd (or perhaps coyote), greyhound, and wolf. It is not recognized by the AKC, however, it is gaining in popularity even outside of Texas. There is also a "Red Lacy." The Blue Lacy is the state dog of Texas.

bluetick coonhound: (not capitalized)

Border collie: (partially capitalized) Breed got its name (probably) from the Scottish Borders where it was bred, and the Welsh word for coal, which is *collie*. Border collies are often named the most intelligent dog breed.

Border terrier: (partially capitalized) Probably named after the *Scottish Borders* area where the dog has been associated with the Border Hunt for decades.

borzoi: (not capitalized) Bred in Russia and similar to the greyhound, the borzoi comes from a Russian word meaning "fast."

Boston terrier: (partially capitalized)

Bouvier des Flandres: (partially capitalized) The French name for the breed means "dog of Flanders." Flanders is a region in Belgium.

boxer: (not capitalized) Bred originally in Germany.

Boykin spaniel: (partially capitalized) Bred in South Carolina and named after Lemuel Whitaker Boykin.

Bracco Italiano: (capitalized) Originating in Italy, the dog is a cross between a German pointer and a bloodhound. "Bracco Italiano" translates to "Italian pointer" but because Italian is one of the languages where the adjective follows the noun, as in *casa blanca* (white house), that dictates "Bracco" should be capitalized, although if translated to English, it wouldn't be.

Briard: (capitalized) Breed came from France and is thought to have originated in the *Brie* region where it got its name.

Brittany: (capitalized) The breed got its name from the region in France.

Brussels griffon: (partially capitalized) Named after Brussels, Belgium, where it originated.

bull terrier: (not capitalized)

bulldog: (not capitalized)

bullmastiff: (not capitalized)

cairn terrier: (not capitalized) Bred in Scotland and used for chasing prey among the cairns (a place where stones are used as burial markers or as markers for a path).

Canaan dog: (partially capitalized) Named after the Canaan region of Israel. The Canaan dog is one of the pariah dogs, or scavengers that survive by living off human settlements.

cane corso: (not capitalized) None of the dictionaries listed the entry as capitalized, but you could argue a case for capitalization. The dog gets its name from the Italian *cane*, which means "dog," and *corso*, which means "Corsican." If we follow the guidelines we set down, it would be fully capitalized because *cane* precedes *corso*.

Cardigan Welsh corgi: (partially capitalized) The name derives from Wales and the Cardigan region of Wales. Corgi is Welsh for "dwarf."

Cavalier King Charles spaniel: (partially capitalized) Originated in England.

Cesky terrier: (partially capitalized) The breed originated in Czechoslovakia where it gets its name.

Chesapeake Bay retriever: (partially capitalized) Originated in the region of the Chesapeake Bay, United States.

Chihuahua: (capitalized) Got its name from the region in Mexico.

Chinese crested: (partially capitalized) Bred in China.

Chinese Shar-Pei: (partially capitalized) From China. The Chinese word *sā pèih*, translates to "sand skin."

Chinook: (capitalized) Breed began in New Hampshire and was named after a sled dog named *Chinook*.

Chow Chow: (not capitalized) From China, originated there thousands of years ago.

Clumber spaniel: (partially capitalized) Originally bred in England. The name comes from Clumber Park.

cocker spaniel: (not capitalized) Originated in England. The word *cocker* refers to the breed's use to hunt woodcocks.

collie: (not capitalized) There is enough confusion over the origin of the name to keep it lowercase. Some say it came from a Scottish word for coal, and some say it derived from a name given to the sheep in the mountainous regions of Scotland. Either way, it would be lowercase.

curly-coated retriever: (not capitalized)

dachshund: (not capitalized) The name is of German origin and means "badger dog."

Dalmatian: (capitalized) I'm probably going to draw a lot of criticism on this, but I'll give my reasons. Presuming the breed originated in Dalmatia, then the name *dalmatian* should be capitalized (according to the guidelines). However, new evidence (irrefutable evidence) suggests the *dalmatian* may have originated in Egypt or the Middle East.

If that's the case, it nullifies the capitalization, or does it? Just because something doesn't hail from a region, doesn't mean it can't be named after that region.

There seems to be a lot of confusion and disagreement on this among the dictionaries. Look at the two definitions below: one is from *Merriam-Webster Unabridged* and the other from *Merriam-Webster Collegiate.*

Merriam-Webster Unabridged

Dal·ma·tian

dalmatian also Dalmatian dog or dalmatian dog : a large dog of a breed supposed to have originated in Dalmatia having a white short-haired coat with black or brown spots varying from dime to half-dollar size, standing from 19 to 23 inches high, and weighing from 35 to 50 pounds — called also coach dog

---

Merriam-Webster Collegiate

---

dal·ma·tian

any of a breed of medium-sized dogs having a white short-haired coat with many black or brown spots

---

As you can see, the Unabridged version lists it both ways: capitalized and not, and the Collegiate version lists it as lowercase.

Merriam-Webster Concise Encyclopedia

I decided to check one more Merriam-Webster source to see how they'd weight in.

dalmatian

Breed of dog named after the Adriatic coastal region of Dalmatia, its first definite home. The time and place of the breed's origin are unknown. Though it has served as a guard dog, war dog, fire-department mascot, hunter, shepherd, and performer, it became best known as a coach or carriage dog, functioning as an escort and guard for horse-drawn vehicles. Sleek and short-haired, it is distinguished by its dark-spotted white coat. It stands 19–23 in. (48–58.5 cm) high and weighs 50–55 lbs (23–25 kg), and is generally even-tempered and friendly.

Misused Words New World Dictionary lists it as shown below:

Dal•ma•tian

Dalmatian

(dalmā´shən)

    adj. of Dalmatia or its people —n. 1 a person born or living in Dalmatia, esp. a Slavic-speaking one 2 a Romance language formerly spoken in Dalmatia 3 any of a breed of large, short-haired dog with black or liver-colored spots on a white coat

---

Oxford English lists it as (capitalized)

Dalmatian

    A dog of a white, short-haired breed with dark spots.

Vocabulary.com lists it as lowercase, but Dictionary.com capitalizes it.

    There is enough confusion about the dog's origin to keep the controversy alive for a long time, however, there isn't much confusion about the origin of the name. Everyone seems to agree that the dog breed is named after the Dalmatian region of Croatia. And since it's named after the region—regardless of whether it came from there—I think it should be (capitalized) The rule says if a breed is named after a region to capitalize it. It doesn't say the breed has to have originated in the region.

    If a person's ancestry shows they came from Italy, it doesn't matter if they were born in England, Ireland, or Australia. When asked about their ethnicity, they would say *Italian*, not *italian*. The same logic applies to *Dalmatian*.

Not to beat a dead horse, but I checked with several dictionaries I often use on my iPad. Here are the results.

- Advanced English Dictionary = lowercase
- Dictionary = uppercase
- One Look = lowercase

Compare this to "Great Dane." The breed supposedly originated in Germany, yet the name derives from Denmark (Dane), but it is still (capitalized)

The thing to take from this non-agreement is what we've said all along. Select a source as your dictionary and stick with it. Do the same for style guides.

That issue took a lot of words, but Dalmatians are popular dogs, and I wanted to get it right.

Dandie Dinmont terrier: (partially capitalized) The breed is named after a fictional character (Dandie Dinmont) in Sir Walter Scott's novel. And yes, we do capitalize if something is named after a character. Look at "Achilles' heel" or "Achilles' tendon."

Doberman pinscher: (partially capitalized) The breed originated in Germany, and it was named after Karl Friedrich Dobermann. The name *pinscher* is German for "terrier."

Dogue de Bordeaux: (capitalized) The breed is descended from the mastiffs and was originally developed in the region of Bordeaux, France. In order to remain consistent, we capitalize *Dogue*.

Capitalizing it also avoids confusion; otherwise it could be mixed up with *any* dog from Bordeaux. This specifies the breed.

English cocker spaniel: (partially capitalized) From England.

English foxhound: (partially capitalized) From England.

English setter: (partially capitalized) From England.

English springer spaniel: (partially capitalized) From England (see notes under Welsh springer spaniel).

English toy spaniel: (partially capitalized) From England.

Entlebucher mountain dog: (partially capitalized) The breed is similar to the Bernese mountain dog, and it comes from the Entlebuch region of Switzerland.

field spaniel: (not capitalized)

Finnish lapphund: (partially capitalized) From Finland.

Finnish spitz: (partially capitalized) From Finland.

flat-coated retriever: (not capitalized)

French bulldog: (partially capitalized) From France.

German pinscher: (partially capitalized) From Germany.

German shepherd dog: (partially capitalized) From Germany.

German shorthaired pointer: (partially capitalized) From Germany.

German wirehaired pointer: (partially capitalized) From Germany.

giant schnauzer: (not capitalized)

Glen of Imaal terrier: (partially capitalized) Named after the Glen of Imaal in western Ireland.

golden retriever: (not capitalized)

Gordon setter: (partially capitalized) From Ireland. Got its name from the Duke of Gordon.

Great Dane: (capitalized) Name derives from Denmark. The *Great* portion is capitalized because it precedes the proper noun, and the capitalization is used to avoid clarification.

Great Pyrenees: (capitalized) Named for the Pyrenees Mountains.

Greater Swiss mountain dog: (partially capitalized) From Switzerland.

greyhound: (not capitalized) Originated in Europe.

harrier: (not capitalized) From England.

Havanese: (capitalized) Got its name from the capital city of Cuba—Havana.

Ibizan hound: (partially capitalized) Named after Ibiza, in the Balearic Islands, Spain.

Icelandic sheepdog: (partially capitalized) From Iceland.

Irish red and white setter: (partially capitalized) From Ireland.

Irish setter: (partially capitalized) From Ireland.

Irish terrier: (partially capitalized) From Ireland.

Irish water spaniel: (partially capitalized) From Ireland.

Irish wolfhound: (partially capitalized) From Ireland.

Italian greyhound: (partially capitalized) From Italy.

Jack Russell terrier: (partially capitalized) Also known as the Parson Russell terrier. The breed takes its name from Reverend John Russell of England.

Japanese Chin: (capitalized) Evidence suggests that the breed originated in China (hence the *Chin* in the name) and was given as a gift to the Japanese emperor.

Keeshond: (capitalized) Supposedly the breed was named for the Dutch rebel—Cornelis (Kees) de Gyselaer—by combining *Kees* with *hound*.

Kerry blue terrier: (partially capitalized) From Ireland, and the name comes from the Kerry Mountains.

Komondor: (capitalized) The breed was brought to Hungary by Cumans, the Turks who settled in Hungary during the 12th and 13th centuries. The name Komondor derives from "Koman-dor," meaning "Cuman dog."

Kuvasz: (capitalized) Though alternative theories exist, the one that seems likely is that the breed may have been named for the Chuvasz people of Russia who bred them for generations. The breed is accredited as having originating in Hungary.

Labrador retriever: (partially capitalized) Originated in Canada and England. Name comes from Labrador, Canada. Color variations occur and there are several established colors: Yellow Lab, Chocolate Lab, and Black Lab. Since *Lab* is merely a shortening of *Labrador,* and since the colors precede the proper noun, I would suggest capitalizing all of them.

Lakeland terrier: (partially capitalized) From England's Lake District, where it gets its name.

Leonberger: (capitalized) Name comes from Leonberg, Germany.

Lhasa apso: (partially capitalized) Name is derived from its origins being in Tibet. Lhasa is the capital city of Tibet, and *apso* means "bearded."

lowchen: (not capitalized) *Lowchen* means "little lion" in German.

Maltese: (capitalized) From the island of Malta in the Mediterranean Sea.

Manchester terrier: (partially capitalized) From England, notably the Manchester region of England.

mastiff: (not capitalized) Mastiffs date back thousands of years and likely originated in Central Asia.

miniature bull terrier: (not capitalized) From England.

miniature pinscher: (not capitalized) Originated in Germany.

miniature schnauzer: (not capitalized) Originated in Germany.

Neapolitan mastiff: (partially capitalized) Name comes from Naples, Italy.

Newfoundland: (capitalized) Named after Newfoundland, Canada.

Norfolk terrier: (partially capitalized) From England. Named after Norfolk county.

Norwegian buhund: (partially capitalized) From Norway.

Norwegian elkhound: (partially capitalized) From Norway.

Norwegian lundehund: (partially capitalized) From Norway.

Norwich terrier: (partially capitalized) From England and named after Norwich.

Nova Scotia duck tolling retriever: (partially capitalized) From Nova Scotia, Canada.

Old English sheepdog: (partially capitalized) From England.

otterhound: (not capitalized)

papillon: (not capitalized)

Parson Russell terrier: (partially capitalized) From England. The breed takes its name from Reverend John Russell who began the breed in the late 18th century.

Pekingese: (capitalized) The breed originated in China and got its name from Peking.

Pembroke Welsh corgi: (partially capitalized) Originated in Pembrokeshire, Wales.

Petit Basset Griffon Vendeen: (capitalized) The name derives from the Vendée region of France. The rest of the name is purely descriptive: *petit* meaning "small," *basset* meaning "low to the ground," and *griffon* referring to "wire-haired." In keeping with the policy of capitalizing words preceding proper nouns, we need to capitalize everything.

pharaoh hound: (not capitalized) Legends say the breed may be descended from dogs of ancient Egypt (hence the pharaoh name), but it hails from the island of Malta where it is used for rabbit hunting.

Plott: (capitalized) From North Carolina. The breed is named after Johannes Plott of Germany, who emigrated to North Carolina in the 1700s.

pointer: (not capitalized)

Polish Lowland sheepdog: (partially capitalized) Named after the Polish Lowlands region.

Pomeranian: (capitalized) Named for the Pomerania region of Poland and Germany.

poodle: (not capitalized) Name may have derived from the German word *pudel* which can be roughly translated to mean "splash in water."

Portuguese podengo pequeno: (partially capitalized) From Portugal. The name *podengo* may refer to the type of hunting dog, and *pequeño* refers to the size (smallest of three).

Portuguese water dog: (partially capitalized) From Portugal.

pug: (not capitalized) Originated in China.

puli: (not capitalized) From Hungary.

Pyrenean shepherd: (partially capitalized) Breed originated in France and is named after the Pyrenees Mountains.

redbone coonhound: (not capitalized)

Rhodesian ridgeback: (partially capitalized) From Rhodesia (now Zimbabwe).

Rottweiler: (capitalized) From Germany and named after the Rottweil region.

Russell terrier: (partially capitalized) See "Jack Russell terrier" or "Parson Jack Russell terrier."

Saluki: (capitalized) One of the oldest purebred breeds, the Saluki hails from the Middle East. It's possible that the name comes from from the ancient Yemeni city of Saluk or from the Syrian city of Seleukia.

Samoyed: (capitalized) From Russia. The breed name comes from the Samoyedic people of Siberia.

schipperke: (not capitalized) The name may come from the people of Brussels referring to it as *chipper*, meaning "shepherd," which makes *schipperke* mean "little shepherd."

Scottish deerhound: (partially capitalized) From Scotland.

Scottish terrier: (partially capitalized) From Scotland.

Sealyham terrier: (partially capitalized) The breed was developed at Sealyham House, overlooking the Sealy River in Wales.

Shetland sheepdog: (partially capitalized) Name from the Shetland Islands off Scotland.

shiba inu: (not capitalized) From Japan. The name "shiva-inu" means "little brushwood dog."

shih tzu: (not capitalized) Originating in either China or Tibet, the name translates to "little lion."

Siberian husky: (partially capitalized) From Siberia.

silky terrier: (not capitalized) Developed in Australia.

Skye terrier: (partially capitalized) Originating on the Isle of Skye in Scotland.

smooth fox terrier: (not capitalized)

Soft Coated Wheaten terrier: (partially capitalized) From the Wheaten region in Ireland.

Spinone Italiano: (capitalized) From Italy. Same reasoning as "Bracco Italiano."

St. Bernard: (capitalized) From Switzerland. Named after the Great St. Bernard Pass in the Alps between Switzerland and Italy.

Staffordshire bull terrier: (partially capitalized) From Staffordshire, England.

standard schnauzer: (not capitalized) Bred in Germany.

Sussex spaniel: (partially capitalized) From Sussex, England.

Swedish vallhund: (partially capitalized) From Sweden. *Valhund* means "herding dog."

Tibetan mastiff: (partially capitalized) From Tibet.

Tibetan spaniel: (partially capitalized) From Tibet.

Tibetan terrier: (partially capitalized) From Tibet.

toy fox terrier: (not capitalized)

treeing walker coonhound: (not capitalized)

vizsla: (not capitalized) From Hungary. *Vizsla* means "pointer."

Weimaraner: (capitalized) The name comes from the Duke of Saxe-Weimar-Eisenach, Karl August, whose court was located in the city of Weimar, Germany.

Welsh springer spaniel: (partially capitalized) From Wales. This is another confusing entry. *Merriam-Webster Collegiate* lists it as partially capitalized , but the *Unabridged* version lists the entry as capitalized, and I have no explanation as to why. Look at the entries below:

Unabridged

Welsh Springer Spaniel *noun*

: a Welsh breed of red and white or orange and white small-eared springer spaniels somewhat smaller and more active than the English springer

Collegiate

Welsh springer spaniel *noun*
    : any of a breed of red and white relatively small-eared springer spaniels of Welsh origin

Collins Dictionary and Vocabulary.com both had it listed as (partially capitalized)

*W*elsh terrier: (partially capitalized) From Wales.

West Highland white terrier: (partially capitalized) From the West Highlands of Scotland.

whippet: (not capitalized) Originated in England.

wire fox terrier: (not capitalized)

wirehaired pointing griffon: (not capitalized)

Xoloitzcuintli: (capitalized) The breed originated with the Aztecs, and the Aztecs are also where it got its name. *Xolotl* was the god of lightning and death, and *itzcuintli* means "dog."

Yorkshire terrier: (partially capitalized) From the Yorkshire region of England.

This concludes the capitalization of dog breeds. It doesn't cover every breed, but it does deal with the ones recognized by the AKC as well as a few others. If you have any questions, please email me.

Chapter Twenty-Two

DONKEY BREEDS

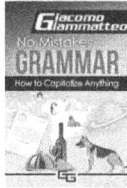

*A*byssinian Donkey: (capitalized) Named after the Abyssinian region of Ethiopia.

American mammoth jack: (partially capitalized) From North America.

Amiatina: (capitalized) The breed originated in Italy, near *Monte Amiata* (Mount Amiata), which is where it got its name.

Anatolia Donkey: (capitalized) Named after the Anatolian region of Turkey.

Andalusian donkey: (partially capitalized) From the Andalusia region of Spain.

Asinara donkey: (partially capitalized) A breed of feral donkeys indigenous to Asinara Island off the coast of Sardinia, Italy.

Asno de las Encartaciones: (capitalized) The breed comes from Spain and is named for the *comarca* of *Las Encartaciones*.

Balearic donkey (also known as the '*Asno Balear*'): (partially capitalized) The breed originated on the Balearic Islands off the coast of Spain.

Balkan donkey: (partially capitalized) Originated in the Balkans of Europe.

Bourbonnais donkey: (partially capitalized) From the Bourbonnais region of France.

Bulgarian donkey: (partially capitalized) From Bulgaria.

burro: (not capitalized) Burros are typically feral donkeys, living in less-populated regions of Mexico, the Southwestern United States, and the Iberian Peninsula. *Burro* is the Spanish word for *donkey*.

Castel Morrone donkey: (partially capitalized) From Italy, originating in the Castel Morrone region of Campania.

Catalan donkey: (partially capitalized) Breed comes from Catalonia, Spain.

Corsican donkey: (partially capitalized) From Corsica, off the coast of Italy.

Cotentin donkey: (partially capitalized) From the lower Normandy region, specifically the Cotentin region, of France.

Cyprus donkey: (partially capitalized) From the Mediterranean island of Cyprus.

Damascus: (capitalized) Named after Damascus, Syria.

Egyptian donkey: (partially capitalized) From Egypt.

English donkey: (partially capitalized) Despite the name, the donkey is bred in Australia.

Georgian ass: (partially capitalized) Originated in Georgia (Asia).

Grigio Siciliano: (capitalized) From Sicily and found in several provinces including Agrigento.

Irish donkey: (partially capitalized) From Ireland.

Jordanian donkey: (partially capitalized) From Jordan.

large standard: (not capitalized)

Libyan: (capitalized) From Libya.

majorera donkey: (not capitalized) The name derives from *majorero*, a word for the people of Fuerteventura, the island it inhabits.

Maltese donkey: (partially capitalized) From the Mediterranean island of Malta.

mammoth jack stock: (not capitalized) From America.

Martina Franca donkey: (partially capitalized) Originated in Southern Italy, near the commune of Martina Franca.

Mary donkey: (partially capitalized) The breed originated in Turkenmenistan in the *Mary* region.

miniature donkey: (not capitalized) One of three donkey breeds recognized as being from the United States.

Miranda donkey: (partially capitalized) The Miranda is a breed that originated in the Terra de Miranda region of northeast Portugal.

Moroccan: (capitalized) From Morocco, Africa.

Norman donkey: (partially capitalized) From the Normandy region of France.

Pantesco: (capitalized) From the island of Pantelleria off the coast of Sicily.

Poitou donkey: (partially capitalized) Originated in the Poitou region of France.

Ponui donkey: (partially capitalized) From Ponui Island off the coast of New Zealand.

Provence donkey: (partially capitalized) From southeastern France, in the Provence region.

Pyrenean donkey: (partially capitalized) From the Pyrenees Mountain region of southern France near the border with Spain.

Ragusano donkey: (partially capitalized) From Ragusa in Sicily.

Romagnolo donkey: (partially capitalized) The breed originated in the Emilia-Romagna region of Italy.

Romanian donkey: (partially capitalized) From Romania.

Sardinian donkey: (partially capitalized) From the island of Sardinia, off the eastern coast of Italy.

spotted donkey (sometimes called a spotted ass): (not capitalized) One of three recognized U.S. breeds. (An *ass* is a male donkey.)

standard donkey: (not capitalized) The *mid-sized* donkey of the U.S. breed. The other sizes are the miniature and mammoth.

Sudanese pack: (partially capitalized) From Sudan.

Syrian: (capitalized) Originated in Syria.

Tadzhikskaya: (capitalized) Got its name from Tajikistan, in Asia.

Thuringian Forest donkey: (partially capitalized) Breed originated in the Thuringian Mountains in the southern part of Thuringia, Germany.

Tibetan: (capitalized) From Tibet.

Tswana: (capitalized) From Africa and named after Botswana.

Tunisian: (capitalized) From the North African country of Tunisia.

Turkmenskaya: (capitalized) Named for the country where it originated, Turkmenistan.

Viterbese: (capitalized) From the town and province of Viterbo, in Italy.

Xinjiang: (capitalized) Originated in the Xinjiang province of China.

Zamorano-Leonés: (capitalized) Breed comes from the provinces of Zamora and León, in Spain.

Chapter Twenty-Three

GOAT BREEDS

The goat, along with sheep, is one of the earliest domesticated animals. Unlike sheep, goats easily revert to feral or wild condition given a chance. In fact, the only domestic species which will return to a wild state as rapidly as a goat is the domestic cat, which explains the large number of feral cats, although the pig rivals both species in its ability to adapt to a feral state.

Abaza: (capitalized) From Turkey and named after the Abaza people of that region.

Adamello blond: (partially capitalized) From Italy and takes its name from the Adamello section of the Alps.

Agew: (capitalized) From Ethiopia and takes its name from the Agaw people who live there.

agrupación de las mesetas: (not capitalized) From Spain and nearly extinct.

Algarvia: (capitalized) From Portugal and named after the Algarvia region of Portugal.

aljabal alakhdar: (not capitalized) From Oman.

Alpine: (capitalized) From France and named after the Alps.

Altai mountain: (partially capitalized) From Russia and named for the Gorno-Altai region.

American Cashmere: (capitalized) From America. It is debatable whether to capitalize *cashmere*. Some dictionaries capitalize it when referring to the "Cashmere goat," but not when using it to describe something, as in "He bought her a cashmere coat."

I think either way would work, and you'd have authoritative resources to back you up. And once again *Merriam-Webster* came through by disagreeing with itself. In the *Merriam-Webster Unabridged*, "Cashmere goat" is capitalized, but in the *Merriam-Webster Collegiate* it is lowercase. See the screenshots that follow (below or next page).

Cashmere goat *noun*

: KASHMIR GOAT

Origin of **CASHMERE GOAT**

from *Cashmere*, region

First Known Use: 1850

cashmere goat *noun*

: an Indian goat raised especially for its undercoat of fine soft wool that constitutes the cashmere wool of commerce

First Known Use of CASHMERE GOAT

1850

I would adhere to the following rule. If referring to the "Cashmere goat," capitalize *Cashmere* because the name derived from *Kashmir*, in India and Pakistan. If referring to *cashmere* as a descriptor of the wool, leave it lowercase, as the name refers to the wool of the goat.

- American Heritage Dictionary lists it as lowercase.
- Vocabulary.com lists the region as uppercase, but the wool as lowercase.
- Dictionary.com lists only the wool (lowercase) and not the goat.

Anglo-Nubian (Nubian): (capitalized) From *Anglo* and *Nubia*.

Angora: (capitalized) Originated in the district of Angora in Asia Minor.

Appenzell: (capitalized) From Switzerland, the Appenzell region.

Arapawa Island: (capitalized) From New Zealand and named for Arapawa Island off the tip of the southern isle.

Australian goat: (partially capitalized) From Australia.

Bagot: (capitalized) From England, dating back hundreds of years. The breed was named after John Bagot, who supposedly received the breed stock from King Richard II.

Barbari: (capitalized) From India, the breed got its name from Berbera, a coastal city located on the Indian ocean.

beetal: (not capitalized) From India.

Belgian fawn: (partially capitalized) From Belgium.

Benadir: (capitalized) From Africa and named for the Benadir region of Somalia.

bhuj: (not capitalized) From Brazil.

Bilberry: (capitalized) From Ireland and the name derives from Bilberry Rock.

Black Bengal: (capitalized) From the Bengal region of Southeastern Asia.

boer: (not capitalized) Name comes from the Dutch word for "farmer." From South Africa.

brown shorthair: (not capitalized) From the Czech Republic.

Canary Island: (capitalized) Named after the Canary Islands.

Canindé: (capitalized) From the Canindé region of Brazil

Carpathian: (capitalized) Name comes from the Carpathian Mountains.

Chamba: (capitalized) Named for the Chamba Upper RIver Valley in the Himalayas.

chamois coloured goat: (not capitalized) From Switzerland.

Changthangi: (capitalized) From India and Pakistan near the Kashmir rgion. These goats are generally domesticated and are reared by nomadic communities called the Changpa in the Changthang region.

chengde polled: (not capitalized) From China, near the Kashmir region of India.

Corsican: (capitalized) From Corsica.

damani: (not capitalized) From Pakistan.

Damascus: (capitalized) Name from Damascus, in Syria.

Danish landrace: (partially capitalized) From Denmark.

Don: (capitalized) Name derives from the Don River in Russia.

duan: (not capitalized) From China.

Dutch landrace: (partially capitalized) From the Netherlands.

Dutch Toggenburg: (capitalized) Breed is from the Netherlands and also derives its name from the Toggenburg region of Switzerland.

Erzgebirge: (capitalized) The breed originated in the Erzgebirge district of Saxony, Germany.

fainting: (not capitalized) The breed is from the United States, and its name comes from the tendency for the goat to temporarily freeze when it panics or feels threatened.

Finnish landrace: (partially capitalized) From Finland.

Frisa Valtellinese: (capitalized) From Italy and from the Valtellina region.

Garganica: (capitalized) From Italy. The breed originated on the Gargano promontory in the Puglia region of southern Italy.

Girgentana: (capitalized) From Italy, and the breed is from the province of Agrigento, in the southern part of Sicily.

Golden Guernsey: (capitalized) From England, and the name comes from the island of Guernsey, in the Channel Islands.

grigia molisana: (not capitalized) From Italy's Campobasso region.

grisons striped: (not capitalized) From Switzerland.

Hailun: (capitalized) From China and found in the region of Heilongjiang.

Haimen: (capitalized) From the Haimen region of China.

hasi: (not capitalized) From Albania.

Hejazi: (capitalized) From the Hejaz region of Saudi Arabia.

Hexi Cashmere: (capitalized) From Mongolia and China. Going with the capitalization of Cashmere when used as a breed of goat and with capitalizing words preceding the proper noun, both words are (capitalized)

Hongtong: (capitalized) From the Hongtong province of China.

huaipi: (not capitalized) The name comes from Chinese meaning "central plain."

Huaitoutala: (capitalized) From China, and the name likely derives from the Huaitoutala district where they graze.

Hungarian improved: (partially capitalized) From Hungary.

Icelandic: (capitalized) Named after Iceland.

Irish: (capitalized) From Ireland.

Jamnapari: (capitalized) From India, and the name is derived from the rivers Yamuna, Jamuna (West Bengal) and Jamuna (Bangladesh) of India and Bangladesh.

Jining grey: (partially capitalized) From the Jining region of China.

jonica: (not capitalized) From the Puglia region of Italy.

Kaghani: (capitalized) From the Kaghan Valley of Pakistan.

Kalahari red: (partially capitalized) From South Africa. The name derives from the color of their coat and the Kalahari Desert.

Kalbian: (capitalized) From Australia, and the name derives from the Kalbian Farm where it was developed.

kamori: (not capitalized) Originated in Pakistan.

kiko: (not capitalized) From New Zealand. Kiko is the Maori word for "flesh."

kinder: (not capitalized) From the United States, using stock from Africa.

Korean black goat: (partially capitalized) From Korea.

kri-kri: (not capitalized) From the island of Crete, the *kri-kri* is a feral goat that naturally inhabits the island.

La Mancha: (capitalized) Originally from La Mancha, Spain.

Laoshan: (capitalized) Name derived from the Laoshan district in China.

majorera: (not capitalized) From the Canary Islands.

Malabari goat: (partially capitalized) From the Malabar region of India.

Maltese: (capitalized) Name comes from the island of Malta.

Markhoz: (capitalized) From the Markhoz district in Iran.

Massif Central: (capitalized) From France. The breed is named after the Massif Central region.

Messinese: (capitalized) From Sicily and named after the province of Messina.

Mini Oberhasli: (capitalized) A U.S. breed that is named after the Oberhasli district in Switzerland.

mountain goat: (not capitalized)

moxotó: (not capitalized) From Brazil.

Murcia-Granada: (capitalized) Named after the Murcia and Granada regions of Spain.

Murciana: (capitalized) Named after the Murcia region of Spain.

nachi: (not capitalized) From the Punjab region of India.

Nera Verzasca: (capitalized) Named after from the Valle Verzasca, in the canton of Ticino in southern Switzerland.

Nigerian dwarf: (partially capitalized) Named after Nigeria.

Nigora goat: (capitalized) An American breed whose name is derived from Nigeria.

Norwegian: (capitalized) From Norway.

Oberhasli: (capitalized) From the Oberhasli district in Switzerland.

orobica: (not capitalized) Originated in Northern Italy.

peacock: (not capitalized) From Switzerland.

Philippine: (capitalized) From the Philippines.

Pinzgauer: (capitalized) Name derives from the Pinzgau region of Austria.

Poitou: (capitalized) Named for the Poitou region of France.

Pridonskaya: (capitalized) It is probable, but not confirmed, that the name comes from the Pridonskaya region of Russia.

pygmy: (not capitalized) Originally from Africa, but now bred in America as well.

pygora: (not capitalized) The pygora resulted from cross-breeding the pygmy goat with the Angora.

Pyrenean: (capitalized) Name comes from the Pyrenees Mountains at the border of France and Spain.

Qinshan: (capitalized) Named after the Qinshan region of China.

red boer: (not capitalized) From South Africa.

Red Mediterranean: (capitalized) Named after the Mediterranean Sea.

repartida: (not capitalized) From Brazil. I couldn't find a source to confirm this, but the meaning seems to translate to "widely spread."

Rove: (capitalized) From France, and the name came from the Le Rove region.

Russian white: (partially capitalized) From Russia.

Saanen: (capitalized) The breed takes its name from the Saanental region in the southern part of Switzerland.

Sable Saanen: (capitalized) Bred in the United States. See above for naming.

Sahelian: (capitalized) From the Sahel region of North Africa.

San Clemente Island: (capitalized) Name comes from the San Clemente Islands off California's coast.

Sarda: (capitalized) From Sardinia.

Short-eared Somali: (capitalized) From Somali.Sirohi: (capitalized) From India. The original breeding tract of Sirohi goat was the Sirohi district of Rajasthan.

Somali: (capitalized) From Somalia.

Spanish: (capitalized) From Spain.

stiefelgeiss: (not capitalized) From Switzerland.

surati: (not capitalized) From India.

Swedish landrace: (partially capitalized) From Sweden.

Syrian mountain goat: (partially capitalized) From Syria.

tauernsheck: (not capitalized) From Austria.

Thuringian: (capitalized) Name comes from Thüringen, in Central Germany.

Toggenburg: (capitalized) From the Toggenburg region of Switzerland.

Uzbek black: (partially capitalized) From Uzbekistan.

Valais blackneck: (partially capitalized) From Valais in Southern Switzerland.

Valdostana: (capitalized) From North Italy, in the Aosta region.

Verata: (capitalized) Originated in the town of La Vera in Spain.

West African dwarf: (partially capitalized) From West Africa.

white shorthaired: (not capitalized) From the Czech Republic.

Xinjiang: (capitalized) Named from the mountains of Xinjiang in China.

Xuhai: (capitalized) From Xuhai, China.

zalawadi: (not capitalized) From India.

zhongwei: (not capitalized) From China.

Chapter Twenty-Four

HORSE BREEDS

*L*isting of horse breeds taken from Wikipedia and the Oklahoma State University Breeds of Livestock.

Abyssinian: (capitalized) Originated in Abyssinia kingdom of Africa.

Akhal-Teke: (capitalized) Capitalization of this one is debatable. *Akhal* refers to a line of oases in the northern part of Turkmenistan, and *Tekke* is the name of a tribe that inhabits the area.

Albanian: (capitalized) Named after Albania, in Europe.

Altai: (capitalized) Named after a mountain range in Asia.

American cream draft: (partially capitalized) From America.

American creme and white: (partially capitalized) From America.

American walking pony: (partially capitalized) From America.

Andalusian: (capitalized) Named after Andalusia in Spain.

Andravida: (capitalized) Named after a region in Greece.

Anglo-Kabarda: (capitalized) Named after part of the Kabardino-Balkaria region of Russia.

Appaloosa: (capitalized) Named after the Palouse River that runs through what was once Nez Perce country. The name evolved into *Apalouse*, and then *Appaloosa*.

Araappaloosa: (capitalized) It is a cross between the Arabian and Appaloosa breeds.

Arabian: (capitalized) Named after Arabia.

Ardennes: (capitalized) Named after a region in France: The Ardennes.

Argentine criollo: partially capitalized due to *Argentine* deriving from Argentina.

Asturian: (capitalized) Named after the Asturias region of Spain.

Australian brumby: partially capitalized due to *Australian*.

Australian stock horse: (partially capitalized) *Australian* is (capitalized)

Azteca: (capitalized) Named after the Aztecs of Mexico.

Balearic: (capitalized) Named after Balearic Islands

Baluchi: (capitalized) Named after a breed of horse native to the Baluchistan, Sindh and Punjab Provinces in Pakistan.

Banker: (capitalized) Named so because it lives on barrier islands in North Carolina's Outer Banks.

ban-ei: (not capitalized) A horse named after *ban-ei*, a form of Japanese horse racing.

barb: (not capitalized) Possibly named after the berbers, a tribe in Northern Africa where the horse may have originated.

Bashkir: (capitalized) Named after the Bashkir people from Russia.

Bashkir curly: (partially capitalized)

basotho pony: (not capitalized) The exact heritage of the horse is not known, but it may have been Arabian.

Belgian: (capitalized) From the Brabant region of Belgium.

bhirum pony: (not capitalized) Also called the Nigerian pony.

bhotia pony: (not capitalized) Comes from Nepal and Northern India.

Boer: (capitalized) From the Boers of South Africa.

Bosnian mountain horse: (partially capitalized) After Bosnia.

Breton: Often (capitalized) Named after the *Brittany* region of the United Kingdom.

buckskin: (not capitalized) Named for the color of skin.

Budyonny: (capitalized) Named after Marshall Semyon Budyonny, a military commander.

Byelorussian harness horse: (partially capitalized) Comes from the region of Byelorussia, Russia.

Calabrese: (capitalized) Named for the Calabria region of Southern Italy.

calvinia horse: (not capitalized) From South Africa.

Camargue horse: (partially capitalized) Named after the Camargue region of Southern France.

Camarillo white horse: (partially capitalized) Named after Adolpho Camarillo, who started the line in 1921.

campeiro: (not capitalized) Of mixed Spanish and Portuguese stock through Brazil.

Campolina: (capitalized) Named after Cassiano Campolina, who developed the breed in the 1850s.

Canadian cutting horse: partially capitalized (Canadian).

Canadian horse: partially capitalized (Canadian).

Canadian pacer: partially capitalized (Canadian).

Canadian rustic pony: partially capitalized (Canadian).

Canadian sport horse/Canadian Hunter: partially capitalized (Canadian).

Canadian warmblood: partially capitalized (Canadian).

canik: (not capitalized) Breed that originated in ancient Turkey.

Carolina marsh tacky: partially capitalized (Carolina). "Marsh tacky" refers to swampy areas of the Carolinas.

Carpathian pony: (partially capitalized) Named after the Carpathian Mountains in Romania.

carthusian horse: (not capitalized) Ancient breed from Spain.

Caspian: (capitalized) Named after the Caspian Sea, where it ran wild in the area surrounding the sea.

Castilian horse: (partially capitalized) Named after the Castilians from Castile.

Catria horse: (partially capitalized) Named for the Catria region in Italy.

Cayuse pony: (capitalized) Named after Cayuse Indian tribe in Oregon.

Celtic pony: (capitalized) From the Exmoor region of the United Kingdom.

cheval demi sang du centre: (not capitalized)

Cerbat mustang: (partially capitalized) Named after the Cerbat Mountain area of Arizona.

certisino: (not capitalized) Descended from the Spanish Andalusion horse.

chahou post pony: (not capitalized) Breed originated in China.

Chaidamu pony: (partially capitalized) Name from the Chaidamu family in Mongolia.

chakouyi: (not capitalized) Ancient breed from China.

Chalosse pony: (partially capitalized) Named after the Chalosse region in France.

champagne horse: (not capitalized) It is not named after the Champagne region but for its color, which is similar to champagne (a pale orange-yellow to light-grayish-yellowish brown).

chamurthi: (not capitalized) One of only four recognized breeds from India. Possibly from Tibet earlier.

chapman horse: (not capitalized) Now extinct breed from England.

charentais: (not capitalized) From France. Also known as the Selle Français horse.

Charollais: (capitalized) Bred in the Charolles region of France.

Charysh/Chara: (capitalized) Named for the Chara River in Russia.

Cheju pony: (partially capitalized) The breed comes from the Cheju Island off the coast of Korea.

Cheval d'Auvergne: (capitalized) Named after the Auvergne region of France.

cheval de corlay: (not capitalized) Breed from Brittany region of France.

Chickasaw horse: (partially capitalized) Named after the Chicksaw Indians.

Chicksaw pony: (partially capitalized) Named after the Chicksaw Indians.

Chilean corralero: (partially capitalized) Breed from Chile.

chilkow: (not capitalized) Breed originated in Russia.

Chilote pony: (partially capitalized) From the Chiloe Island off southern Chile.

Chincoteague pony: (partially capitalized) There are several theories on how the name developed, but many associate it with nearby Chincoteague Bay.

Choctaw horse: (partially capitalized) Named for the Choctaw Indian tribe.

Chumbivilcas horse: (partially capitalized) Thought to have been named after the Chumbivilcas Province.

Chumysh horse: (partially capitalized) Breed from near the Chmysh river in the Altai region of Russia.

chyanta pony: (not capitalized) The horse is native to Nepal.

cimarron horse: (not capitalized) The cimarron is not a recognized breed, but any horse that has gone feral and become wild.

Cleveland bay: (partially capitalized) Comes from the Cleveland area of Northern England.

Clydesdale: (capitalized) Originated in Clyde Valley in Scotland.

cob: (not capitalized)

Coffin Bay pony: (partially capitalized) A breed native to Coffin Bay, on the southern tip of the Eyre Peninsula in Australia.

coldblooded trotter | coldblood traveling rail: (not capitalized) From Norway.

Colonial Spanish: (capitalized) From Spanish settlers in America. *Colonial* is part of the name just like "Great" is part of "Great Dane" or "Great Pyrenees."

Colorado Ranger: (capitalized) Some suggest keeping this partially capitalized and some have suggested keeping *Ranger* capitalized to ensure clarity since *ranger* is also an occupation, but the dictionary has it lowercase. According to our capitalization policies, we would keep *ranger* lowercase, but I have no problem making an exception for a situation such as this; it's logical.

comtois horse: (not capitalized) Breed came to France from Germany around 4th century.

Conestoga horse: (partially capitalized) Controversy surrounds this naming. Supposedly the horses were so named because of their use to pull the *Conestoga* wagons, however, the wagons were name after Conestoga River in PA. (or the Conestoga township) so the horse breed name should be (capitalized)

Connemara pony: (partially capitalized) Originated in the Connemara region of Western Ireland.

corajoso/courage pony: (not capitalized) Breed is from Brazil

Corolla Island pony: (partially capitalized) Named after Corolla, NC., where the horses live wild on the Outer Banks.

Corsican horse | Corsica horse: (partially capitalized) Name comes from the island of Corsica, in the Mediterranean.

cossak horse: (not capitalized) Originally from Russia.

Costa Rican saddle horse: (partially capitalized) From Costa Rica.

country saddle horse: (not capitalized) Breed originated in Kentucky and formed part of the bloodline for the Tennessee walker.

Cretan horse: (partially capitalized) Originally from the isle of Crete off the coast of Greece.

criollo: (not capitalized) Breed name originated in Argentina.

crioulo: (not capitalized) Breed is similar to the criollo and is found to have originated in the southern part of Brazil.

Crioulo Brasileiro | curraleiro: (capitalized) Brasileiro is capitalized because it stems from Brazil; *criollo* is capitalized because it precedes *Brasileiro* as a name element.

Croatian hladnokrvnjak: (partially capitalized) After Croatia.

Croatian posavac: (partially capitalized) From the flood plains in Croatia by the Sava River.

Cuban paso: (partially capitalized) Cuba has no native horses, so these horses came from the Spanish settlers.

Cuban pinto: (partially capitalized) Cuba has no native horses, so these horses came from the Spanish settlers.

cukurova: (not capitalized) Originally bred in Turkey.

curly horse: (not capitalized)

curly haired fox trotter: (not capitalized)

Cutchi: capitalized The breed takes its name from the region of Kathiawar in India where it originated.

Czech coldblood: (partially capitalized)

Czechoslovakian small riding horse: (partially capitalized)

Czech warmblood: (partially capitalized)

Dagestan pony: (partially capitalized) From the coastal plains of Dagestan, Russia.

Dahoman: (capitalized) Named after an Arabian stallion named *Dahoman*.

dales pony: (not capitalized) Comes from England near the Scottish border.

deliorman | deliormanski: (not capitalized) From Bulgaria.

Danish sport pony: (partially capitalized) Breed comes from Denmark.

Danish Wamblood: (partially capitalized) Breed comes from Denmark.

Danube Delta horse: (capitalized) Name comes from the Danube Delta in Romania.

Danubian | Dunav: (capitalized) From the Danube River area.

darashouri | darashouli: (not capitalized) Originally from Iran, and not much else is known.

Darfur pony: (capitalized) Breed comes from the southern Darfur region of Sudan.

dartmoor pony: (not capitalized) From England.

Datong horse: (capitalized) Horse is native to the Datong River basin in the northern Qinghai Province of China.

Debao pony: Often (capitalized) May have been named after Debao County, a region of China.

Deli pony: (capitalized) Name originally came from the port of Deli, India where they were exported to Indonesia, which is now the recognized location of the breed.

Desert Norman horse: (partially capitalized) From Normandy, France. I'll stick with capitalizing *desert* since it precedes the proper noun and may be considered as a title would.

Deutsches reitpony: (partially capitalized) Often called the German riding pony.

dilbaz | deliboz | daliboz | delibozskaya: (not capitalized) Breed is from Azerbaijan.

djamoi | djamonský pony: (not capitalized) From Indonesia.

djerma horse: (not capitalized) From Niger in Western Africa.

døle gudbrandsdal | dølehest | døle trotter: (not capitalized) From Norway.

dolny-iskar: (not capitalized) Extinct breed from Bulgaria.

Don | Donskaya: (capitalized) Developed on the steppes by the Don River in Russia.

Dongola | Dongolah | Dongolawi: (capitalized) The Dongala breed is thought to have come from the Dongala Providence in Sudan.

dosanko horse: (not capitalized) Breed comes from the Japanese island of Hokkaido.

drum horse: (not capitalized) From England where they are often used in events and parades.

dülmen pony: (not capitalized) From Germany.

Dutch draft: partially capitalized due to *Dutch*.

Dutch harness horse: partially capitalized due to *Dutch*.

Dutch warmblood: partially capitalized due to *Dutch*.

dzhabe: (not capitalized) From Kazakhstan.

East Bulgarian horse: (partially capitalized) In order to be consistent, we'll keep *East* capitalized since it precedes a proper noun.

East Friesian horse: (partially capitalized) Name is thought to have come from *Frisia*, a region on the coast of Germany and the Netherlands.

East Friesian warmblood: (partially capitalized) Name is thought to have come from *Frisia*, a region on the coast of Germany and the Netherlands.

East Prussian: (capitalized) Breed originated in Eastern Prussia.

Edelbluthaflinger: (capitalized) Takes its name from the village of Haflinger in Austria, near the Tyrol Mountains.

Ege Midillisi: (capitalized) Native to Midillisi island off the coast of Turkey where it gets its name.

Egyptian Arabian | Egyptian horse: (capitalized) Both names are proper nouns: Egypt and Arabia.

Einsiedler: (capitalized) The breed is named for the Benedictine Abbey of Einsiedeln where it has been bred for hundreds of years.

Eleia: (capitalized) Thought to be named after the Eleia part of Greece, where it comes from.

English thoroughbred: (partially capitalized) I'm going to go with capitalizing *English* but not *thoroughbred*. I realize this may create a stir, as many, many sites list *thoroughbred* as always being capitalized, however, I didn't find a reason why, and the rules would indicate that it should not be (capitalized) (See my notes under *thoroughbred* for more detail.)

Equus Kinsky: (capitalized) Got their name from Count Kinsky, who originally bred them. Going with our policy of capitalizing the part of the name that precedes the proper noun, we'll keep *Equus* capitalized as well. The horse came from the Czech Republic.

Equus Przewalskii: (capitalized) Named after a Russian explorer named Colonel Przewalski. They are native to Mongolia.

Eriskay pony: (partially capitalized) Thought to be named after Eriskay Island off the coast of Scotland.

erlanbach: (not capitalized) Extinct breed from Switzerland.

erlunchun: (not capitalized) Old breed from China.

Esperia pony: (partially capitalized) Named for Esperia, which is south of Rome.

Estonian draft | **Estonian arden:** (partially capitalized) Named after *Estonia*.

Estonian native: (partially capitalized) Named after *Estonia*.

Exmoor pony: (partially capitalized) Thought to have been named from the Exmoor Forest where they often roamed.

Faroe pony | **Faeroes pony** | **Faeroe Island horse:** (capitalized) Named after the Fareoe Islands near Denmark.

Faca Galizana: (capitalized) Named after the Galicia region of Spain.

Falabella: (capitalized) Named after the Fallabella family who developed the breed. From Argentina.

fell pony: (not capitalized) From England.

Finnhorse | **Finnish universal:** (capitalized) Finnhorse is one word, and capitalized due to being named after Finland, where it originated.

Finnish warmblood: (partially capitalized) Named after Finland.

fjord horse: (not capitalized) From Norway.

Flemish horse: (partially capitalized) From South Africa.

fleuve: (not capitalized) Name is French for *river*. The breed is from Senegal.

Flores pony: (capitalized) Thought to be named for the Flores Islands of Indonesia.

Florida cracker horse | **Florida horse** | **Florida cow pony:** (partially capitalized)

foundation quarter horse: (not capitalized) Many people capitalize "Quarter Horse" even though I see no reason to do so based on the rules. *Merriam-Webster* lists it as lowercase, but the Oxford English Dictionary lists it as capitalized with the lowercase as an option.

Fouta horse | Foutanké: (capitalized) Thought to have been named for the Fouta region of Senegal.

Frederiksborg horse: (capitalized) Named after King Frederick of Denmark.

freiberger horse | Franches Montagnes | freiberger: The freiberger is also known as a "Franches Montagnes," and if it is referred to as such it should then be capitalized as that name stems from a district of Switzerland named the same.

French saddlebred/halfblood: (partially capitalized) From France.

French Anglo-Arab: (capitalized)

French Ardennais: (capitalized) From the Ardennes region of France.

French cob: (partially capitalized) From France.

French saddle pony: (partially capitalized) From France.

French sport horse: (partially capitalized) From France.

French trotter: (partially capitalized) From France.

Friesian: (capitalized) Name from the province of Friesland in the Netherlands.

Friesian sporthorse: (partially capitalized) Name from the province of Friesland in the Netherlands.

Furioso horse: (partially capitalized) Named after a horse called *Furioso*.

gala horse: (not capitalized) From Ethiopia.

Galiceño pony: (partially capitalized) From Mexico, mixed with breeds from Spain, notably the Galician which is from Galicia..

Galician pony | Gallego | Galaga: (partially capitalized) Name from Galicia, Spain.

Galloway pony: (partially capitalized) Extinct breed from Scotland, and got its name from the Galloway region.

Galshar: (capitalized) Breed comes from the Galshar area of Mongolia.

garrano | garrano do minho: (not capitalized) Ancient breed from Portugal.

Gayoe pony: (partially capitalized) Name comes from the Gayoe Hills of Sumatra, in Indonesia.

Gelderlander | Gelderland: (capitalized) Name comes from the Gelderland province in Holland.

Georgian grand: (partially capitalized) From Georgia in the United States, and means "Georgian grand" or great.

German coach horse: (partially capitalized) From Germany.

German cold-blooded: (partially capitalized) From Germany.

German riding pony: (partially capitalized) From Germany.

gharbaui: (not capitalized) From Sudan.

gharkaw | Western Sudani: (not capitalized) Also called the "Western Sudan pony" and if used that way, it's (partially capitalized)

Ghazi: (capitalized) Possibly named for the Ghazi Khan district of Pakistan.

giara: (not capitalized) Comes from Sardinia.

Gidran: (capitalized) From Hungary and named after a stud named *Siglavy Gidran.*

Glasinacki: (capitalized) From Bosnia and is named after the village of Glasinac on the Romanija mountain.

Goklan: (capitalized) Thought to be named after the Goklan tribe or region of Turkmenistan.

Golden American saddlebred: (partially capitalized) From America.

Golden Horse of Bohemia | Kinsky horse: fully or

partially capitalized, depending on which name you use. Bohemia is a region of the Czech Republic and Count Kinsky developed the breed.

Gotland pony: (partially capitalized) Native to the Gotland Island of Sweden.

Grand Noir du Berry donkey: (partially capitalized) The Grand Noir of Berry is named from the French region of Berry. "Grand Noir" simply means "big black," however, in keeping with policies, since "Grand Noir" precedes the proper noun, we'll keep it (capitalized)

Grayson Highlands ponies: (partially capitalized) The Grayson Highlands ponies are a herd of semi-feral animals that live in Grayson Highlands State Park in Virginia.

Great Poland horse: (partially capitalized) Early on they were known as the "Poznan Horse," named after Poznan County, in Poland.

Greek pony: (partially capitalized) Comes from Greece.

Groningen horse | Groninger: (partially capitalized) Comes from the northern province of Gronigen in the Netherlands.

Guangxi horse | Guanxi: (partially capitalized) Name comes from the Guangxi Zhuang region of China.

Guanzhong: (capitalized) From the Guanzhong region of China.

Guba: Also called the Azerbaijan horse. (capitalized) Thought to have been named from the Guba region of Azerbaijan.

Guizhou pony: (capitalized) Named after the Guizhou province of China.

Guoxia pony: (partially capitalized) Named after the Gouxia region of China.

gutsul | guculs | guzuls: Also called the "Carpathian

pony." not capitalized as *gutsul,* but if called Carpathian pony, it is (partially capitalized) From Romania. Also see "Hutsul" or "Hucul."

gypsy vanner: (not capitalized) Comes from Ireland.

hackney horse: (not capitalized) From England. Possibly named after the Hackney district in London, but doubtful.

hackney pony: (not capitalized) From England and possibly named after the Hackney district in London, but doubtful.

half-saddlebred: (not capitalized) From America.

Haflinger: (capitalized) Takes its name from the village of Haflinger in Austria, near the Tyrol Mountains.

handachine horse | Also called the kandach: (not capitalized) From Japan, although purebloods no longer exist.

Hanoverian: (capitalized) Thought to have been named for the city of Hanover.

Hantam horse: (capitalized) Probably named after the Hantam municipality of South Africa. Also known as the Calvinia horse, a region in Hantam.

harddraver | Holländischer | hardtdraver: (not capitalized) *Harddraver* is Dutch for trotting horse.

harna | hazziz: (not capitalized) Also known as the *unmol* horse. It is from the northwest Punjab in India.

Hebridean pony: (partially capitalized) Named after the Hebrides Isles off the coast of Scotland.

heck horse: (not capitalized) Also known as the tarpan horse (now extinct) from Russia.

Heihe horse: (capitalized) Comes from the boundary between China & Russia along the Heilongjiang River Basin in Heihe city.

Heilongkiang: (capitalized) From the northern

Heilongkiang province of China (often spelled as Heilongjiang).

henson horse: (not capitalized) Also known as the Somme bay horse. From France.

hequ | hequl: (not capitalized) Previously known as the Nanfan horse. It originated by the Yellow River and the Gansu Province in China.

Hessen horse | Hessischer: (capitalized) From Hesse, Germany.

Highland pony: (partially capitalized) From Scotland—the region known as the Highlands.

Highlander horse: (partially capitalized) From Scotland's Highlands.

Hinis horse | Hinisin Kolu Kisasi Ati: (capitalized) Named after Hinis, a province in Eastern Anatolia (Turkey).

hispano | Hispano Arabe: (not capitalized) From Spain.

hirzai: (not capitalized) From Pakistan.

Hmong horse: (capitalized) Name derived from the Hmong people of Vietnam and Southeast Asia.

Hokkaido pony: (partially capitalized) Name comes from the Japanese island of Hokkaido.

Holsteiner: (capitalized). Named from the Elmshorn district of Holstein.

Holsteiner coldblood: (partially capitalized) Named from the Elmshorn district of Holstein

horse of the Americas: (partially capitalized) From America.

Hrvatski Hladnokrvnjak: (capitalized) Hrvatski is the Croatian name of Croatia.

Hrvatski posavac: (partially capitalized)

Hucul | Huçul | Hutsul | Hutul | Huculska | Huzul :

Also known as the Carpathian pony. (capitalized) Named after the Hutsul people.

Hungarian horse | Hungarian Felver: (partially capitalized)

Hungarian draft | Hungarian coldblood: (partially capitalized)

Hungarian dun: (partially capitalized)

Kabarda: (capitalized) From the Karbadian people of the Caucusus region of Russia.

Kagoshima: (capitalized) Named after a city on the island of Kyushu in Japan.

Kaimanawa horse: (capitalized) Named for the Kaimanawa Mountains in New Zealand.

kaju pony: (not capitalized) From Indonesia.

kaldblodstraver: (not capitalized) From Norway.

Kalmyk: (capitalized) Named after the Kalmyk people of Western Mongolia, near the Russian border. Breed comes from Russia.

kandachi: (not capitalized) Originally from Japan. Purebloods of this breed no longer exist.

Karabair: (capitalized) Probably named after the Karabair, Uzbekistan region.

Karabakh: (capitalized) Named after the Karabakh region of Azerbajain, near Armenia.

Karacabey: (capitalized) The breed originated in the Marmara region of Turkey and was possibly named after Karacabey, a city in that region. The breed has been extinct since 1979.

Karachai: (capitalized) Named after the Karachay region or the Karachay people of the northern Caucasus in Russia.

karakacan: (not capitalized) Breed comes from Turkey.

Kordofani: (capitalized) Breed is named for the region of southwestern Kordofan, Sudan.

Kathiawari: (capitalized) Named after the Kathiawar Peninsula of India.

Kazakh horse: (capitalized) Named for the Kazakh people of Russia.

Ke-Er-Qin: (capitalized) Breed comes from the Keerqin steppe in inner Mongolia.

Kentucky mountain saddle horse: (partially capitalized) Bred in Eastern Kentucky.

Kerry Bog pony: (capitalized) Named after Kerry, Ireland.

Khani: (capitalized) Possibly named after Khani, Pakistan, where the breed originated.

Kiger mustang: (partially capitalized) Name derived from Kiger Island off the coast of Oregon, where the breed originated.

Kinsky horse: (partially capitalized) Named after Count Kinsky, a nobleman from the Czech Republic.

Kirdi pony: (partially capitalized) From Cameroon, where the *Kirdi* are a group of ethic groups who inhabit the northwestern part of Cameroon.

Kirghiz: (capitalized) Probably named after the Kyrgyz people of Turkey.

Kisber Halfbred: (capitalized) Named after Kisber, Hungary.

Kiso horse: (capitalized) Name comes from the Kiso RIver in Japan.

Kladruby horse: (capitalized) Named after the Kladruby region of the Czech Republic.

Kleines Deutsches reitpferd: (partially capitalized)

Kleines refers to the *smallness* of the breed, and *reiptferd* simply means "saddle horse."

klepper: (not capitalized) From Estonia. Also known as the Estonian native horse.

knabstrupper: (not capitalized) From Denmark.

konik horse: (not capitalized) The name means "little horse" in Polish.

Kuda-Gayo: (capitalized) Name comes from the Gayoe Hills region of Sumatra.

Kumingan: (capitalized) Name comes from a town and district located in eastern West Java, Indonesia,

Kundudo: (capitalized) From the Kundudo Mountain region of Ethiopia.

Kushum: (capitalized) Possibly named for the Kushum region of Kazakistan.

Kustanai: (capitalized) Named after the city of Kostanay in Kazakistan.

Kuznetsk horse: (capitalized) Probably named after a town by that name in Russia.

Kyrgyz horse: (capitalized) Named after the people called *Kyrgyz*, in Russia.

KWPN: (capitalized) KWPN is an initialism for Koninklijk Warmbloed Paard Nederland, a Dutch breed.

Landais pony: (capitalized) Name comes from the region of Landes in the southwest of France.

Latgale trotter: (partially capitalized) Named after a region of Latvia.

Latvian: (capitalized) Named after Latvia.

lehmkuhlener pony: (not capitalized)

Leutstetten: (capitalized) Named after a region in Germany.

Lewitzer pony: (not capitalized) From Germany and named after the Lewitz region.

Lichuan: (capitalized) May have gotten its name from the Lichuan region in China.

Lijiang pony: (partially capitalized) Name comes from the Lijiang district in China.

Limousin horse: (partially capitalized) Comes from the Limousin region of France.

Lippit Morgan: (capitalized) Named for the two men who began the breed: Justin Morgan and Robert Lippit Knight.

Lipizzan: (capitalized) Named after the town of Lippizza near the northwest border of Italy close to Austria.

Lithuanian heavy draft: (partially capitalized) From Lithuania.

Lithuanian landrace: (partially capitalized) From Lithuania.

Little Poland horse: (partially capitalized) From Poland. And in keeping consistent with policy, *little* remains capitalized because it precedes the proper noun *Poland.* It's not a little horse from Poland, but a "Little Poland" horse.

Ljutomer trotter: (partially capitalized) From Ljutomer, Slovenia.

llanero: (not capitalized) A llanero refers to a South American herder, taking its name from the *llaños* grasslands. The breed comes from Venezuala.

Lokai: (capitalized) The breed comes from Tadzhikistan, and it takes its name from the Lokai tribe.

Lombok: (capitalized) From the Indonesian island of Lombok.

Losino: (capitalized) From the Losa valley in Spain.

Lundy pony: (partially capitalized) From the Isle of Lundy in England.

Lusitano: (capitalized) Named for the Lusitanian people of early Portugal.

Lyngen horse: (partially capitalized) Got its name from nearby Lyngen in Norway.

Mallorquin horse: (capitalized) From the Spanish island of Mallorca.

malopolski: Also known as the Little Poland horse.

Mangalarga marchador: (partially capitalized) From Brazil. *Mangalarga* refers to the name of the farm where the breed originated, and *marchador* has to do with the breed's accelerated gait. The breed has become very popular and is the national horse of Brazil.

Mangalarga Paulista: (capitalized) Paulista is a region in southern Brazil, and is what the Mangalarga Paulista is named after.

Manipuri pony: (partially capitalized) Named after Manipur, a region of northeastern India.

Maremmano: (capitalized) The Maremmano is a breed of horse originating in the Maremma area of Tuscany and northern Lazio in Italy.

Mecklenburg: (capitalized) Named for the Mecklenburg region in Germany.

Menorca: (capitalized) Named after one of the Balearic Islands owned by Spain.

Merens pony: (partially capitalized) Named after a village in the Pyrenees Mountains.

Messara horse: (partially capitalized) Named after the Mesara Plains in Greece.

Mezen: (capitalized) Named after the Mezen Valley in Russia.

Minusin horse: (partially capitalized) Breed comes from the Minusin Valley in Russia.

Missouri fox trotting horse: (partially capitalized) Developed in the Ozarks.

Miyako horse: (partially capitalized) Comes from the Miyako Islands off Japan.

Miyazaki: (capitalized) The Misaki Pony comes from the Mayazaki Province in Japan

Mongolian: (capitalized) After Mongolia.

Mongolian wild horse: (partially capitalized) Native to Mongolia.

Montana travler: (partially capitalized)

Monterufoli pony: (partially capitalized) Named after the Monterufoli region of Tuscany, Italy.

morab: (not capitalized) Bred in the United States.

Morgan horse: (capitalized) Named after Justin Morgan (Vermont), the original breeder.

Moroccan barb: (partially capitalized) Originally from Morocco.

Moyle horse: (partially capitalized) Named after Rex Moyle of Idaho, the developer of the breed.

mulassier horse: (not capitalized) Also known as the Poitevin horse. *Mulassier* translates to "mule breeder."

Mura: (capitalized) Probably named after the Mura River in Hungary where the breed originated.

Murgese: (capitalized) From the area of Murege, Apulia in Italy.

mustang: (not capitalized) The word mustang comes from the Spanish word, *mestena* which is roughly translated as "a group of wild horses."

Namib Desert horse: (partially capitalized) Found in the Namib Desert of Africa.

Neapolitan: (capitalized) Named after Naples, Italy, where the breed originated.

Nederlands Appaloosa pony: (capitalized) After the Netherlands and the Appaloosa breed.

New Forest pony: (partially capitalized) Native to the New Forest area of England.

New Kirgiz horse: (partially capitalized) Found in the Kirgizia and Kazakistan.

Newfoundland pony: (partially capitalized) Named after Newfoundland.

Nez Perce horse: (partially capitalized) Named after the Nez Perce people of North America.

Nigerian: (capitalized) Named after Nigeria.

Noma horse: (partially capitalized) Originated in Noma County, Japan.

Nonius: (capitalized) The breed was named after the founding sire, *Nonius*, and is from Hungary.

Nooitgedacht pony: (partially capitalized) The breed is one of the only horses indigenous to South Africa. It is named after the Nooitgedacht Research Station nearby.

Nordland horse: (partially capitalized) From Norway.

Norfolk roadster: (partially capitalized) Originated in Suffolk.

Noric: (capitalized) Named after the Noric region of the eastern Alps, near Austria.

Norman cob: (partially capitalized) Named after the Nordland region of Norway.

North African barb: (partially capitalized) Originally bred in North Africa.

Northern Ardennais: (capitalized) Originated in the Ardennes region of France and Belgium. In keeping with policy, *Nothern* remains (capitalized)

Norwegian fjord: (partially capitalized) From Norway.

Norwegian riding pony: (partially capitalized) From Norway.

Norwegian trotter: (partially capitalized) From Norway.

Ob pony: (partially capitalized) Originated in Russia, probably from the Ob River region.

Oberlander horse: (partially capitalized) Name came (perhaps) from the Oberlander Jews who inhabited the northwestern region of Hungary.

Oldenburger: (capitalized) Named after the city of Oldenburger.

Ocracoke: (capitalized) Name came from Oracoke Island off North Carolina.

Old Austrian warmblood: (partially capitalized) In keeping with policy, *Old* remains (capitalized) It helps differentiate between an *old* Austrian warmblood horse, and an "Old Austrian" warmblood horse. The first example is designating the horse as *old*, while the second may refer to a newborn foal of the breed "Old Austrian warmblood." It's the same reasoning that we used with "Old English sheepdog."

Old English black horse: (partially capitalized) Same logic as above.

Orlov-Rostopchin: (capitalized) Developed by Count Orlov of Russia.

Orlov trotter: (partially capitalized) Developed by Count Orlov of Russia.

Oromo horse: (partially capitalized) Named after the Oromo people of Ethiopia.

Outer Banks ponies: (partially capitalized) The breed inhabits and is named after the Outer Banks of North Carolina.

paint horse: (not capitalized) This colorful breed was introduced to American by the Spanish.

palomino: (not capitalized) Breed has specific color requirements.

Pampa horse: (partially capitalized) From Brazil and named after the *pampas*, a vast region of plains in Brazil and stretching into Argentina and Uruguay. *Merriam-Webster* was the only dictionary to list *pampas* as a capitalized entry, but considering it's a geographic place name, I feel it should be.

Pantaneiro: (capitalized) Comes from the Panatanal region of Brazil.

paso fino: (not capitalized) *Paso fino* translates to "fine step," and the breed's unique gait is apparently a genetic trait that hasn't been able to be taught to others. The breed is thought to have originated in Columbia.

Percheron: (capitalized) Thought to have taken their name from the Perche region of western France

Peruvian paso: (partially capitalized) From Peru via the Spanish explorers. Known for its smooth gait.

Persano horse: (partially capitalized) Named after Persano, Italy.

Petiso pony: (partially capitalized) Name probably comes from nearby village in Argentina—Ciervo Petiso.

Pindos pony: (partially capitalized) Named for the Pindus Mountains in Greece.

Pinkafo: (capitalized) Probably named for a nearby city —Pinkafeld.

Pintabian: (capitalized) Name derives from cross-breeding American horses (pintos) with Arabian horses. The name *pintabian* was trademarked in 1994.

Pinzgauer horse: (partially capitalized) Probably came

from the village of Pinzgau in Austria. Also known as the Noric horse.

Piquira pony: (not capitalized) From Brazil.

Pleven: (capitalized) Name likely derived from Pleven, Bulgaria, where the breed originated.

Poitevin: (capitalized) Name comes from the region of Poitu, France, where the language spoken is referred to as Poitevin.

Polesian: (capitalized) Named after the Polesia region of Poland which even goes into Russia. The breed is also known as the Konik.

Polish konik: (partially capitalized) See above.

Pony of the Americas: (capitalized) *Pony* precedes the proper noun.

Posavina horse: (partially capitalized) Developed in the Posavina region of Croatia.

pottok: (not capitalized) Pottok is the Basque language name for the breed which has been in Spain for centuries, living wild in the mountains.

Przewalski's horse: (partially capitalized) This horse is also known as *Equus Przewalskii, Asiatic wild horse,* and *Mongolian wild horse.* It is the only known truly wild horse on the planet and is even considered to be a different species by some, as it has sixty-six chromosomes compared to a normal horse, which has sixty-four. The horse is named after the Russian geographer and explorer Nikołaj Przewalski.

Qatgani horse: (partially capitalized) The Qatagani (or Qataghani) is a breed from the former Qataghan province of Afghanistan.

quarab: (not capitalized) From the United States.

quarter horse: (not capitalized) I know I'll catch hell for not capitalizing this, but it doesn't call for it. "Quarter horses" get their name from the speed they show in a race of a quarter mile or in the first quarter mile they run. It is the largest breed registry in the world, but that still doesn't give it a right to be (capitalized)

quarter pony: (not capitalized) See above.

racking horse: (not capitalized) Developed in the United States (I believe in Alabama) and is derived from the Tennessee walkers.

rahvan: (not capitalized) From Turkey, and its name comes from the Turkish word *rahvan* which is used to describe their gait.

rangerbred horse: (not capitalized) Also known as the *Colorado Ranger* horse.

Rhineland heavy draft: (partially capitalized) Takes its name from the Rhineland region of Germany.

Riwoche pony: (partially capitalized) Named after the Riwoche monastery and/or the town of Riwoche in Tibet. This breed is ancient and is thought by some to be the "missing link" between the ancient wild horses and the horses of today. Because of the isolation of living in Tibet, the bloodline has been pure for centuries.

Rocky Mountain horse: (partially capitalized) Takes its name from the Rocky Mountains.

Romanian saddle horse: (partially capitalized) From Romania.

Romanian trotter: (partially capitalized) See above.

Russian Don: (capitalized) Developed in Russia near the Don RIver.

Russian heavy draft: (partially capitalized) From Russia.

Russian riding horse: (partially capitalized) From Russia.

Russian trotter: (partially capitalized) From Russia.

Sable Island pony: (partially capitalized) From Canada's Sable Island, off the coast of Nova Scotia.

Sachsen warmblood: (partially capitalized) The breed got its name from Sachsen which translates into *Saxony*, a state of Germany.

saddlebred: (not capitalized) Also known as the "American saddlebred." Developed in Kentucky.

Sadecki: (capitalized) Also called the "Little Poland horse." Sadecki may have gotten its name from the mountain range in the eastern Carpathian Mountains near the border.

Salerno horse: (partially capitalized) Also known as the Persano, this horse gets its name from Salerno, Italy.

Samolaco: (capitalized) Thought to be named after the town of Samolaco in Italy, not from from Milan.

sandalwood pony: (not capitalized) From Indonesia and named for one of the country's primary exports: sandalwood.

San Fratello horse: (partially capitalized) Named after San Fratello, a town in Sicily.

sanhe: (not capitalized) Name derives from the Chinese word *sanhe* which means "three rivers," which is where the breed originated—at the confluence of three rivers in Mongolia.

Sardinian: (capitalized) Named after the Italian island of Sardinia.

Saxon-Turinga coldblood: (partially capitalized) Names derive from Saxony and Turinga—regions of Germany.

Saxony warmblood: (partially capitalized) Name from Saxony.

Schleswiger heavy draft: (partially capitalized) Name comes from the Schleswig state of Germany where it meets Denmark.

Schwarzwälder Fuchs: (capitalized) Named after the

region in Germany by the Black Forest. (The horse is sometimes called the Black Forest horse.)

selle Français: (partially capitalized) Selle Francais translates roughly into "French saddle."

selle Français pony: (partially capitalized) See above.

Seminole pony: (partially capitalized) Known by many names: Chicksaw Pony, Seminole Pony, Marsh Tackie, Prairie Pony, Florida Horse, Florida Cow Pony & Grass Gut, but when it's referred to as Seminole pony, it is using the name as acquired from the Seminole Indians.

Senne horse: (partially capitalized) Comes from the Senne region of Germany.

sertanejo: (not capitalized) Developed in Brazil, and descended from the desert horses in North Africa, the name could have come from a Brazilian town called Seraneja, but more likely it derives from the term *sertanejo* which is similar to what we know as a cowboy.

Shackleford Banks horse: (partially capitalized) Named after Shackleford Banks off the coast of North Carolina in the Outer Banks region.

Shagya Arabian: (capitalized) Named after the founding stud: *Shagya*, an Arabian horse that was imported from Syria and into Hungary.

Shan pony: (partially capitalized) Named after the Shan Highlands in Burma.

Shetland pony: (partially capitalized) Named from the Shetland Islands off the coast of Scotland.

shire horse: (not capitalized) Originated in England.

Silesian: (capitalized) Got its name from the Lower Silesia area of Poland.

single-footing horse: (not capitalized) Bred as trail horses in the United States.

Sini: (capitalized) From the Sini River region of China.

Skyros pony: (partially capitalized) From the Skyros Islands off Greece.

Slovak sport pony: (partially capitalized) Originated in Slovakia.

Slovak: (capitalized) Came from Slovakia.

Sorraia: (capitalized) Named after the Sorraia River region of Portugal. It is an ancient breed, dating back thousands of years.

South African miniature: (partially capitalized) From South Africa.

South African vlaamperd: (partially capitalized) From South Africa.

South African warmblood: (partially capitalized) From South Africa.

South German coldblood: (partially capitalized) From Germany.

Soviet heavy draft: (partially capitalized) From Russia (Soviet Union).

Spanish Anglo-Arabian: (capitalized)

Spanish barb: (partially capitalized) From Spain.

Spanish colonial horse: (partially capitalized) From Spain.

Spanish jennet: (partially capitalized) From Spain.

Spanish mustang: (partially capitalized) From Spain.

Spanish Norman: (capitalized) From Spain and (presumably) Normandy, France, as the Percheron was used in the breed.

spiti pony: (not capitalized) From India near the Himalayas. Also known as a chamurthi horse.

spotted saddle horse: (not capitalized) From the United States. So named due to their coloring.

standardbred: (not capitalized) A U.S. breed. Sometimes known as American standardbred.

strelets horse: (not capitalized) The name could have come from a Russian military unit (*strelsky*) that dates back hundreds of years. Despite efforts to save the breed, it is now extinct.

Sudan country-bred: (partially capitalized) From Sudan.

Suffolk punch: (partially capitalized) Suffolk punch got its name from Suffolk, England.

sugarbush draft: (not capitalized) From the United States.

Sulawesi: (capitalized) From the island of Sulawesi in Indonesia.

Sumba pony: (partially capitalized) From the island of Sumba in Indonesia.

Sumbawa pony: (partially capitalized) From the island of Sumba in Indonesia.

Swedish Ardennes: (capitalized) From Sweden and bred with horses from the Ardennes in France.

Swedish warmblood: (partially capitalized) From Sweden.

Swiss warmblood: (partially capitalized) From Switzerland.

Taishuh: (capitalized) From islands in western Japan.

takhi horse: (not capitalized) Also called the Equus Przewalskii, Asiatic Wild horse, Mongolian Wild Horse & Taki. The origin of this horse may predate modern equines.

tarpan: (not capitalized) Now, extinct, this horse may have roamed the Russian Steppes in prehistoric times.

Tavda: (capitalized) Named for the Tavda River Valley in northern Russia.

tawleed: (not capitalized) From Sudan.

Tennessee walking horse: (partially capitalized) From Tennessee in the United States.

Tennuvian: (capitalized) I'll err on the side of caution here. The name Tennuvian stems from combing the two breeds that were used to establish this breed: Tennessee walkers and Peruvian pasos. They combined the first part of Tennessee with the latter part of Peruvian to get the name. Since both words are capitalized when used under normal circumstances, I think we should keep the newly formed word (capitalized)

Tersk: (capitalized) Began on a stud farm in Russia by the name of Tersk Stud Farm.

Thai pony: (capitalized) Comes from Thailand.

Thessalian: (capitalized) Comes from the mountainous regions of Thessaly, Greece.

thoroughbred: I suggest it remain lowercase, but *Merriam-Webster Unabridged* says: usually (capitalized)

When referring to the specific breed of horse, it is capitalized, as in "He's a Thoroughbred horse." However, if using it as an adjective to mean something pure, as in "That's a thoroughbred dog," it is lowercase.

With that said, *Merriam-Webster Collegiate* shows it as lowercase, but says to capitalize it when referring to the breed specifically.

- Oxford English Dictionary lists it as lowercase whether used as an adjective or noun.
- Cambridge dictionary lists it as lowercase.
- Collins dictionary lists it as lowercase.
- Dictionary.com lists it as lowercase, but sometimes

with an initial capital letter when referring to a specific breed.

- Vocabulary.com also lists it as lowercase.

I checked numerous other dictionaries. Most listed it as lowercase, although some capitalized it when referring to the horse breed. I checked with CMOS, and they maintained it should be capitalized when referring to the horse breed to distinguish it from the other meaning of the word (as purebred).

I don't see that as reason enough to break the rule. I suggest keeping it lowercase. If anyone complains, you have Oxford English Dictionary and numerous other resources to back you up.

Tibetan pony: (capitalized) From Tibet.

tiger horse: (not capitalized) Developed in China, and the name relates to the spotted patterns on the horses' coats.

Timor pony: (partially capitalized) From the Indonesian island of Timor.

tinker horse: (not capitalized) From Ireland and named after the tinker wagons they used to pull.

Tokara pony: (partially capitalized) Comes from the Tokara Islands in Japan.

Tolfetano horse: (partially capitalized) Comes from the town of Tolfa, in the mountains north of Rome, Italy.

Tori: (capitalized) Named after the Tori Stud farm in Estonia.

Trakehner: (capitalized) Breed was originally developed at the East Prussian state stud farm in the town of Trakehnen from which the breed takes its name.

Trottatore Italiano: (capitalized) This is a tough one. Policy dictates to capitalize *trottatore* because it precedes a proper noun, however, *trottatore* is simply the Italian word for *trotter*. It is much the same as the dog breed: Bracco Italiano, which means "Italian Pointer," and it is (capitalized)

Tunisian pony: (partially capitalized) From Tunisia.

Turk: (capitalized) From Turkey.

Tyrol pesante rapido: (partially capitalized) It is also known as the Italian heavy draft horse. Name derives from the Tyrol Mountains region of northern Italy and Austria.

Ukrainian saddle-riding horse: (partially capitalized) From Ukraine.

unmol: (not capitalized) Comes from India, where the name means "priceless."

Upper Yenisei: (capitalized) Name comes from the Yenisei River which runs through Russia and Mongolia. It is one of the few major rivers to flow northward, and is the largest river system to flow into the Arctic Ocean.

uzunyayla horse: (not capitalized) From Turkey.

Venezuelan criollo: (partially capitalized) From Venezuela.

Ventasso horse: (partially capitalized) From the Ventasso Mountains in Italy.

Vietnamese hmong: (partially capitalized) From Vietnam.

Virginia highlander: (partially capitalized) Developed in Virginia, United States.

vlaamperd: (not capitalized) The name means "Flenish horse" in South Africa.

Vladimir heavy draft: (partially capitalized) From the Vladimir region of Russia.

Voronezh coach: (partially capitalized) From the Voronezh district in Russia.

Vyatka: (capitalized) May be named after the Vyatka River where the breed originated, in Russia.

Waler: (capitalized) Name comes from New South Wales where they were traded to other countries frequently.

Welara pony: (partially capitalized) This is another example similar to the Tennuvian. This breed is a cross between a Welsh and an Arabian, both of which should be capitalized, so I'll recommend capitalizing the name of *Welara*.

Welsh mountain pony: (partially capitalized) From Wales, one of their oldest breeds.

Welsh pony: (partially capitalized) From Wales.

West African barb: (partially capitalized) Comes from West Africa.

West Norwegian: (capitalized) From the western section of Norway.

Western Sudan pony: (partially capitalized) From Western Sudan.

Westfalen: (capitalized) From Westphalia, in Germany.

Westfalen pony: (partially capitalized) Same as above.

Wielkopolski: (capitalized) Breed gets its name from Wielkopolska, a region in west central Poland.

Wild horses of the Namib: (partially capitalized) These horses are from the Namib, and to differentiate them from "any wild horse from Namib" we should keep it (capitalized)

Württemberger: (capitalized) Comes from Württemberger, Germany.

Xilingol: (capitalized) Comes from the steppes of southeastern Xilinggral Meng, in Mongolia.

yabou: (not capitalized) From Turkmenistan. Name comes from the language and means "a poor man's horse."

Yamud: (capitalized) The Yamud breed is from Turkmenistan and is also known as the *Iomud*. The name comes from the Iomud Tribe in the southern part of Turkmenistan.

Yakut horse: (partially capitalized) I'll presume the name comes from Yakutia, in Russia, since that is where the breed originated. As a side note, they live farther north than any horse breed.

Yemeni horse: (partially capitalized) Comes from Yemen.

Yili horse: (partially capitalized) Developed in the grasslands of the Yili-Kazakh District in China.

Yugoslav mountain pony: (partially capitalized) From Yugoslavia. The breed is also known as the Bosnian pony.

Yorkshire coach horse: (partially capitalized) Named after the Yorkshire region of England.

Yunnan: (capitalized) Named after the Yunnan province in southwest China.

Yururi Island horse: (partially capitalized) Named after Yururi Island in Japan.

Zangersheide: (capitalized) Name comes from the studfarm in Zangersheide, Belgium.

Zaniskari pony: (partially capitalized) Named for the Zanskar Valley region of India.

Zeeland: (capitalized) Named after the province of Zeeland in western Belgium.

Zweibrücker: (capitalized) Named after Zweibruchen, Germany.

Part One

POULTRY BREEDS

Poultry has long been a part of people's lives. Whether it's for eggs or meat or other things: chickens, turkeys, ducks, and geese play a major role in everyday life, so it's no wonder there has been so much time spent on improving the breeds.

Following is a list of recognized breeds for chickens, ducks, geese, guinea hens, and turkeys.

Chapter One

CHICKEN BREEDS

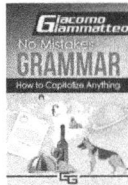

*A*meraucana: (not capitalized) Developed in the United States, the breed used Araucana stock and it resembles the Araucana as well.

Ancona: (capitalized) Originated near Ancona, Italy, where it got its name.

Andalusian: (capitalized) From the Andalusian region of Spain.

Appenzell bearded hen: (partially capitalized) Originated in the Appenzell region of Switzerland.

Appenzell pointed hood hen: (partially capitalized) Originated in the Appenzell region of Switzerland.

Araucana: (capitalized) From Chile and name derives from the Araucanía region.

aseel: (not capitalized) From India, where *aseel* means "high born."

Australorp: (capitalized) Developed in Australia from Black Orpington stock, which was named after the town of Orpington.

Baheij: (capitalized) Named after the closest town to the research station that developed the breed in Egypt.

Bandara: (capitalized) Named after the village of Bandara near a research center in Egypt.

Barnevelders: (capitalized) Named for the Barneveld region of Central Holland.

Brahmas: (capitalized) The breed can be traced back to China, but the name derives from the Brahmaputra River in India.

Buckeye: (capitalized) Developed in Ohio and named after the state's nickname—Buckeye.

buttercup: (not capitalized) From Sicily.

Campine: (capitalized) From the region of La Campine, Belgium.

Catalana: (capitalized) The breed originated in Catalonia, in Eastern Spain.

Chantecler: (capitalized) The breed was created by a monk in Montreal, Canada, Brother Wilfrid Chatelain, and named after a poem, "Chantecler" by Edmond Rostand, a French poet.

cochin: (not capitalized) From China. Originally known as "Cochin-Chinas." If referred to as "Cochin-Chinas," then it's fully (capitalized)

Cornish: (capitalized) Developed in the Cornwall region of England.

Crevecoeur: (capitalized) The name is derived from a town, "Creve-Coeur en Ange," in the Normandy providence of France.

Cubalaya: (capitalized) From Cuba.

Delaware: (capitalized) From the state of Delaware, United States.

dominiques: (not capitalized) The breed originated in

Québec, Canada, but now they are predominantly bred in the United States.

Dorking: (capitalized) Originally brought to England by the Romans, and breeding began near the town of Dorking.

Dutch Bantam: (capitalized) From the Netherlands and from Bantam Island off the coast.

Faverolles: (capitalized) The breed's name comes from the small village in which it was found, Faverolles, a town in the region of Eure-et-Loire, France.

Frieslands: (capitalized) From the Frisia region of Germany.

frizzle: (not capitalized) Possibly originated in Asia.

Gimmizah: (capitalized) Developed at the El-Gimmizah Poultry Research Farm in Egypt.

Golden Montazah: (capitalized) Developed at the Montazah Poultry Research Farm in Egypt.

gray jungle fowl: (not capitalized) This breed was a wild ancestor of the domesticated chickens and was found in the jungles of India.

green jungle fowl: (not capitalized) Same as above: the breed was a wild ancestor of the domesticated chickens and found in the jungles of India.

Hamburgs: (capitalized) The breed is thought to have originated in Holland, but the name likely came from Hamburg, Germany.

Holland: (capitalized) From Holland.

Houdan: (capitalized) Named for its area of origin, the village of Houdan, in France.

Java: (capitalized) The breed was developed in the United States, but stock from Asia and other areas were used. It is suspected the name came from the island of Java, where some of its ancestors may have come from.

Jersey giant: (partially capitalized) Developed in New Jersey.

La Fleche: (capitalized) The breed gets its name from the town of La Fleche, east of Paris, France.

Lakenvelder: (capitalized) The breed originated in Holland, and its name may derive from the village of Lakerveld.

Lamona: (capitalized) Developed in the United States by Harry Lamon, where it got its name.

Langshan. The breed may have gotten its name from the nearby town of Langshan or from Mount Langshan, in China.

legbar: (not capitalized) Created in England.

leghorn: (not capitalized) Created in England.

Marans: (capitalized) Takes its name from Marans, France.

Malay: (capitalized) From Malaysia.

Matrouh: (capitalized) A region in Egypt near where it was developed.

Minorca: (capitalized) Developed in Spain, and the name comes from Minorca Island off the coast.

modern game: (not capitalized) Developed in England.

naked neck (Turken): (not capitalized) From Romania.

nankin: (not capitalized) Bred in England, but the name is thought to have derived from the color of nankeen cotton from China.

New Hampshire red: (partially capitalized) From New Hampshire.

Old English game: (partially capitalized) From England.

Orpington: (capitalized) Developed in Orpington, England.

Plymouth Rock: (capitalized) Developed in Mass-achusetts and named after Plymouth Rock.

Polish: (capitalized) From Poland.

red cap: (not capitalized) From England.

Rhode Island red: (partially capitalized) Rhode Island and the New England states are where the breed was developed. I don't know why, but the *Red* portion of the name is capitalized in every resource I checked, with the exception of the Word Web Dictionary, which had it lowercase. Word Web had it listed as shown below:

Rhode Island red
 ***(pl.* Rhode Island reds)**

American breed of heavy-bodied brownish-red general-purpose chicken

Gallus gallus, chicken

According to all guidelines by CMOS and AP, it should be lowercase, but CMOS even uses it in one of their examples, and they show it uppercase, but with no explanation as to why. Without a logical reason for the capitalization of *red*, I am keeping it lowercase.

I wrote to both CMOS and AP looking for reasons why this would be (capitalized) Below is the question I sent followed by the responses:

My question

Why is "Rhode Island Red" shown with the "Red" capitalized? It seems to go against recommendations by all style guides of capitalizing only the proper nouns or name elements that precede them (not follow them).

AP's response

AP doesn't have a specific style. I see that Webster's New World College Dictionary (which you may get as part of your Stylebook subscription) uses Rhode Island Red, as does Merriam-Webster. I can't speak to their reasoning for sure, but I imagine it's for clarity to distinguish from a general reference to the color.

CMOS's response

"Rhode Island Red," as the name of a specific breed of domestic chicken, is considered to be a proper name.

CMOS's response was not only worthless, it was wrong. It not only goes agains their rules, it goes against most of the breeds they take the time to recognize. Look at the following from *Merriam-Webster*, CMOS's dictionary of choice.

Colorado ranger noun
Definition of *Colorado ranger*
: a parti-colored horse of a breed developed in the

western U.S. by interbreeding barbs with native stock
ultimately of Spanish origin

That is the name of a specific breed as are hundreds more
that aren't (capitalized) And if there might be any confusion,
it would more likely be with *Colorado ranger* than it would with
Rhode Island Red. A Colorado ranger could easily be mixed up
with a human who lives in Colorado and has an occupation as
a ranger.

Or how about . . .

- *Tennessee walker?*
- Douglas fir
- red cedar
- Kentucky coffee tree
- Kentucky mountain saddle horse

Russian Orloff: (capitalized) The breed was originally
developed by Count Orloff of Russia.

Sebright: (capitalized) Developed in England by Sir John
Sebright.

shamo: (not capitalized) The breed was brought to Japan
from Thailand. The name *shamo* is thought to be a corruption
of the name *Siam* (modern day Thailand).

silkie (bantam): (not capitalized) From China. The bird
was so named because the fur was said to feel like silk.

Silver Montazah: (capitalized) Developed in Egypt at
the Montazah Poultry Research Farm.

Styrian: (capitalized) Originating in Austria and nearby
Slovenia in the Styria region.

sultan: (not capitalized) Originating in Turkey, the name translates from Turkish as "fowl of the sultans."

Sumatra: (capitalized) From Sumatra.

Sussex: (capitalized) From Sussex, England.

Swiss hen: (partially capitalized) From Switzerland.

White-Faced Black Spanish: (capitalized) From Spain.

Welsummer: (capitalized) From the village of Welsum, in Holland.

Wyandottes: (capitalized) Developed in the United States in upstate New York, the name stems from the Wyandotte Nation that inhabited that area.

Yokohama: (capitalized) From Yokohama, Japan.

Chapter Two

DUCK BREEDS

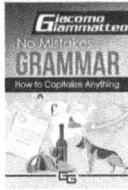

Call: (not capitalized) Call ducks were originally used to lure wild ducks toward hunters with their calls, however, that practice disappeared with the invention of duck calls.

Cayuga: (capitalized) The breed originated in New York and is named after Lake Cayuga.

crested: (not capitalized) The crested duck has been around for hundreds of years, perhaps originating in Holland.

Khaki Campbell: (capitalized) The breed was developed by Adele Campbell, from England, during the late 1800s. The khaki name may have come from the duck's coloring. Like all breeds, *khaki* is capitalized because it precedes the proper noun.

muscovy: (not capitalized) Despite the similarities, there is no logical reason to assume the name derives from the *Muscovy* region of Russia. Some have suggested ties to a trading company, but there isn't evidence to support that theory.

Orpington: (capitalized) Developed by William Cook of England, the same man who developed the Orpington chicken.

Pekin: (capitalized) This breed originally came from Germany and was bred with stock from China, which is likely where the name came from (the old city of Peking).

Pommeranian duck: (partially capitalized) The name derived from Pomerania.

rouen: (not capitalized) Originally from France. The name came from Brits referring to them as "Rhones" meaning they were from the Rhône River region of France. Eventually, it corrupted into *rouen*.

runner: (not capitalized) The breed originated in Indonesia. They do not fly, instead, they walk or (if in a hurry) run to the market.

Chapter Three

GEESE BREEDS

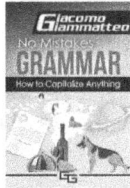

*A*frican: (capitalized) From Africa.

Chinese: (capitalized) From China.

Diepholz: (capitalized) The Diepholz Goose comes from Northern Germany, from the county named Diepholz.

Egyptian: (capitalized) From Egypt.

Embden: (capitalized) The breed originates from Emden (formerly Embden), Germany.

pilgrim: (not capitalized) Developed in England and supposedly arrived in America with the pilgrims.

Pomeranian: (capitalized) From the Pomerania region of Germany.

Toulouse: (capitalized) Developed in southern France, near Toulouse.

Chapter Four

GUINEA HEN BREEDS

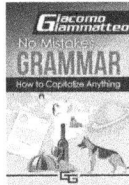

Guinea fowl: (partially capitalized) The wild Guinea fowl from West Africa (Guinea) is regarded as the original of the domestic stock.

Chapter Five

TURKEY BREEDS

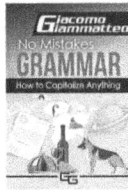

TURKEY BREEDS

black: (not capitalized) Developed in Europe from turkeys brought back from Mexico.

Bourbon: (capitalized) Developed in Bourbon County, Kentucky.

bronze: (not capitalized) Developed in the United States. It gets its name from the bronze coloring.

Narragansett: (capitalized) Developed in Narragansett Bay, Rhode Island.

royal palm: (not capitalized) Developed in Florida.

slate: (not capitalized) Developed in the United States. It gets its name from the slate-gray coloring.

white: (not capitalized) Developed in Mexico and imported by Holland. The breed is sometimes known as the Holland white.

Chapter Twenty-Five

SHEEP BREEDS

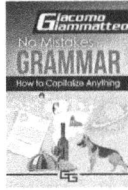

Many people don't think of sheep breeds regarding issues dealing with capitalization, but sheep have been around for a long time, and there are a lot of breeds to consider—many of them named after the place of origin.

acipayam: (not capitalized) From Turkey. The name *acipayam* means "bitter almond."

adal: (not capitalized) From Ethiopia.

Afghan Arabi: (capitalized) Name derives from Afghanistan and Arabia.

Africana: (capitalized) Name derives from Africa.

Alai: (capitalized) From Kyrgyzstan and the Alai Mountain region where the sheep derive their name.

Alcarrena: (capitalized) The breed originated in Spain in the La Alcarria region.

algarvechurro: (not capitalized) Sometimes seen as two words: *algarve churro*. Bred in southern Portugal.

Algerian Arab: (capitalized) Name comes from Algeria and Arabia.

Altay: (capitalized) From China, originating in the Altway Mountains region.

American blackbelly: (partially capitalized) From America.

Apennine: (capitalized) Name derives from the Appenine Mountains of Italy.

Arabi: (capitalized) Name from Arabia.

Arapawa Island: (capitalized) Name comes from Arapawa Island off New Zealand.

Awassi: (capitalized) The breed name is often attributed to the "El Awas" tribe who lived in the Tigris River region.

Balkhi: (capitalized) Originated in Afghanistan and Pakistan. The breed is thought to have gotten its name from Balkh, a city in Afghanistan.

Baluchi: (capitalized) From Afghanistan and Pakistan and thought to have gotten its name from the nearby Balkh in Afghanistan.

Balwen Welsh mountain: (partially capitalized) Originating in Wales, the name *balwen* comes from Welsh and translates to "blazing white." Because it precedes the proper noun, we keep it (capitalized)

Barbados blackbelly: (partially capitalized) Breed originated from the island of Barbados. It is sometimes seen spelled as "Barbados black belly."

Bavarian Forest: (capitalized) Name from the Bavarian Forest.

Bentheimer landschaf: (partially capitalized) From Germany and named after the Bentheim region.

Bergamasca: (capitalized) Breed is from Italy, and it is named for the town of Bergamo.

beulah speckled-face: (not capitalized) From Wales. *Possibly* from near a town called Beulah, but not confirmed.

bibrik: (not capitalized) From Pakistan.

Biellese: (capitalized) From the Piedmont region of Italy, specifically, the Biella region where it derives its name.

Blackhead Persian: (capitalized) From Persia.

Black Welsh mountain sheep: (partially capitalized) From Wales and Welsh Mountains. *Mountain* is not capitalized because the sheep are named after the color of the breed: see picture below. They are not named for the *Welsh Black Mountain*, or the *Welsh Black Mountains* that lie north and west of that.

bleu du Maine: (partially capitalized) From the Maine et Loire Mayenne region of the southern part of France.

Bluefaced Leicester: (capitalized) Name from the Leicestershire region of England.

Bond: (capitalized) Developed in Australia and named after Thomas Bond.

Booroola merino: (partially capitalized) Developed by brothers from Booroola, Australia.

Border Leicester: (capitalized) From the Leicester region.

Boreray: (capitalized) The breed originated on the Scottish island of Boreray.

Bovska: (capitalized) The breed derives its name from the small town Bovec in upper Slovenia near the Italian border.

braunes bergschaf: (not capitalized) From Austria and the nearby parts of Italy.

Brazilian Somali: (capitalized) From Brazil and deriving its name from Brazil and Somalia.

Brecknock Hill Cheviot: (capitalized) From the United Kingdom, specifically the Brecknock Hill region and the Cheviot range of hills to the north.

British milk sheep: (partially capitalized) From England.

brillenschaf: (not capitalized) From Austria. The name *brillenschaf* means "sheep with glasses," referring to the dark coloration around the breed's eyes.

Bündner Oberland: (capitalized) From Switzerland and named after the Bündner Oberland region.

California red: (partially capitalized) From California.

California variegated mutant: (partially capitalized) From California.

Campanian barbary: (partially capitalized) Breed is from Campania, Italy.

Castlemilk moorit: (partially capitalized) From Scotland and deriving its name from the Castlemilk estate where they were bred. *Moorit* simply refers to the coloring in their faces.

Charollais: (capitalized) From the Charollais region of France.

Cheviot: (capitalized) From England and Scotland. The name refers to the highest point in the Cheviot Hills.

Chios: (capitalized) From Greece and named after Chios, one of the larger Greek islands.

Cholistani: (capitalized) From Pakistan and named after the Cholistan Desert.

Clun Forest: (capitalized) Originating from the Clun Forest area of England and Wales.

Coburger fuchsschaf: (partially capitalized) From Germany and drawing its name from Coburger.

columbia: (not capitalized) Bred in the United States.

comeback: (not capitalized) Bred in Australia.

Comisana: (capitalized) Named after Comiso in Sicily.

Coopworth: (capitalized) Developed in New Zealand and subsequently Australia, the name came from Ian Coop, who developed the breed.

Cormo: (capitalized) Name comes from the crossing of Corriedale sheep and merino sheep. Breed originated in Australia.

Corriedale: (capitalized) Australia was the initial home to this breed, where it got its name from a piece of land in the South Island.

Cotswold: (capitalized) Originated in the Cotswold Hills of England.

criollo: (not capitalized) Developed in South America, primarily Columbia.

Dala: (capitalized) From Norway. The breed name may derive from the Dalarna province of nearby Sweden.

Damani: (not capitalized) From Pakistan.

Damara: (capitalized) From Namibia, and the name derives from the Damaraland region.

Danish landrace: (partially capitalized) From Denmark. *Landrace* simply means "improved breed."

Dartmoor: (capitalized) From England. *Dartmoor* is a moor in southern Devon, which is where the sheep got their name.

Debouillet: (capitalized) Breed comes from New Mexico and is a cross between Rambouillet and Delaine Merino.

Delaine merino: (partially capitalized) I made an assumption that *Delaine* is a person's name or a place name. I spent hours researching the origin of the *Delaine* portion of the name and couldn't find any information pointing to the name's origin.

Merriam-Webster had the breed listed as an entry, but they had both words (capitalized) OED didn't have it listed, but it had *merino* listed as lowercased.

Derbyshire gritstone: (partially capitalized) Native to England and from the Derbyshire region.

Devon closewool: (partially capitalized) Breed originated in England as a cross between a Devon and Exmoor ewes.

Deutsches blaukoepfiges fleischschaf: (partially capitalized) Bred in Germany.

Dorper: (capitalized) A breed developed in South Africa by crossing the Dorset horn, which originated in England, with the Blackhead Persian.

Dorset: (capitalized) Bred in England. The breed came from Dorsetshire.

Dorset down: (partially capitalized) From Dorsetshire, England.

Drysdale: (capitalized) The name derives from Dryfesdale, a location in Lanarkshire, New Zealand.

Elliottdale: (capitalized) Developed in Australia at the Elliott Research Station in Tasmania.

Exmoor horn: (partially capitalized) Developed in Exmoor, Devon (England).

Fabrianese: (capitalized) From the town of Fabriano in the Marche region of Italy.

Faeroes: (capitalized) From the Faroe Islands off the coast of Denmark.

Finnsheep: (capitalized) Native to Finland.

Fonthill merino: (partially capitalized) From Australia, the Fonthill region of Tasmania.

Friesian milk sheep: (partially capitalized) From the Friesland region of Germany.

Galway: (capitalized) From the Galway region of Ireland.

Gansu alpine fine-wool: (partially capitalized) From Gansu Province, China.

gentile di Puglia: (capitalized) From the northern part of Puglia, in Italy. No need for capitalization of the words preceding Puglia because there is a *di* which means *of,* eliminating the potential for confusion.

German blackheaded mutton: (partially capitalized) From Germany.

German mountain: (partially capitalized) From Germany.

German mutton merino: (partially capitalized) From Germany.

German whiteheaded mutton: (partially capitalized) From Germany.

Gotland sheep: (partially capitalized) Named for the Swedish island of Gotland.

Graue gehoernte heidschnucke: (not capitalized) From Germany. *Heidschnucke* means "moorland sheep," and "graue gehoernte" means "gray horned."

gromark: (not capitalized) From Australia.

Gulf Coast native: (partially capitalized) Named for the Gulf Coast. From Florida.

Gute: (capitalized) From Sweden and named for Gute on the Gotland Island.

Hampshire: (capitalized) From Hampshire in southern England.

Han: (capitalized) From the Han region of China.

Harnai: (capitalized) From Pakistan. Harnai is the capital of the Baluchistan region.

Hasht Nagri: (capitalized) From Pakistan where they are found in the Hasht Nagar region.

Hazaragie: (capitalized) From Afghanistan and named after the Hazara region of central Afghanistan.

Hebridean: (capitalized) Named after a group of islands off the coast of Scotland.

herdwick: (not capitalized) From England. The breed name comes from old Norse meaning "sheep pasture."

Hill Radnor: (capitalized) From England. The breed got its name from the hills bordering Radnor in Wales.

Hog Island sheep: (partially capitalized) The breed is from Virginia, and the name is derived from Hog Island, one of the barrier islands off Virginia's coast.

Hu: (capitalized) Breed comes from China. It is not verified, but many people think *Hu* is derived from one of several places in China named *Hu*. It is a likely source, but not confirmed.

Icelandic: (capitalized) From Iceland.

Ile-de-France: (capitalized) The breed originated in France and derives its name from a region by that name. It's odd because "Ile-de-France" means "Isle of France," and yet the region lies just north of the center of France and is landlocked.

Istrian pramenka: (partially capitalized) The breed is native to the Istria region of Croatia. It is often known as the "Istrian milk sheep."

jacob: (not capitalized) Breed comes from England. It has been bred there for hundreds of years, and no one seems to know where the name comes from.

Jezersko-Solcava: (capitalized) From Austria and Slovenia. Its name derives from the regions of Jezersko and of Solčava, formerly in the Austrian Empire, now in Slovenia.

Kachhi: (capitalized) Breed is found in the Katchh district of Pakistan.

kajli: (not capitalized) From the Sargodha and Gujrat districts of Pakistan.

Karakul: (capitalized) From Turkey and named after the village of Karakul which lies in the valley of the Amu Darja River. It is believed this breed may be the oldest breed of sheep, dating back to 1,400 B.C or earlier.

Katahdin: (capitalized) The breed was developed in Maine and was named after Mt. Katahdin, the highest point in Maine.

Kerry hill: (partially capitalized) The breed comes from near the border of England and Wales, and derives its name from the village of Kerry, near Newtown.

kooka: (not capitalized) From Pakistan.

Langhe: (capitalized) Breed comes from Italy, near the Piedmont region, specifically near the Langa Hills.

lati: (not capitalized) From Pakistan.

Leicester longwool: (partially capitalized) Breed originated in England and got its name from Leicester.

Leineschaf: (capitalized) From Germany and gets its name from the Leine River Valley.

Lincoln: (capitalized) From England and gets its name from Lincoln, England.

Llanwenog: (capitalized) From Wales and derives its name from Llanwenog, Walels.

Lleyn: (capitalized) From Wales and gets its name from the Lleyn Peninsula of Wales.

lohi: not capitalized Breed was developed in India, in the northern Punjab state where it borders Pakistan. It's possible the name derives from a nearby town in Pakistan (Lohi), but I've found no evidence to verify this.

lonk: (not capitalized) Breed developed in England, and the name *lonk* derived from the old Lancashire word that means *lanky*. Since the sheep were long and thin, they were given the name.

Luzein: (capitalized) From Switzerland and the name from the village Luzein in the Prättigau region.

Manx loaghtan: The Manx breed derives its name from the Isle of Man, and the word *loaghtan* refers to the brown coloring. It comes from the Manx words "*lugh dhoan.*"

Masai: (capitalized) Breed is from Africa and the name derives from the Maasai people of East Africa.

Massese: (capitalized) The breed is named for the province of Massa Carrara, Italy.

medium-wool merino: (not capitalized) The name *merino* has a lot of theories surrounding the origin of its name, but so far none of them have proved conclusive. A couple of dictionaries offer capitalizations as a variant to the lowercased *merino,* but most don't and list it as lowercase only.

Mehraban: (capitalized) The breed originated in Iran, in the Mehraban region.

merinolandschaf: (not capitalized) From Germany.

Moghani: (capitalized) From Iran, and the name derives from the Moghan steppe region.

montadale: (not capitalized) The sheep developed in the United States, but I have found nothing to say where the name originated.

Morada Nova: (capitalized) From Brazil, and the name derives from the Morada Nova region of northern Brazil.

mouflon: (not capitalized) The sheep come from Corsica and are thought to be the ancestors of all domesticated sheep. The name comes from *mufra* and *mufro* which were Corsican words that the people used to refer to males and females.

Navajo-Churro: (capitalized) Breed is from the United States but originally used stock from the Spanish Churras. The name derives from the Navajo Indian tribe and the Churra region of Spain, which is where the Churra breed got its name.

Norfolk horn: (partially capitalized) Found in Norfolk, England, which is where the name comes from.

North Country Cheviot: (capitalized) From Scotland and named after the Cheviot Hills region near the border with England.

Norwegian fur: (partially capitalized) From Norway.

Old Norwegian: (capitalized) From Norway.

Orkney: (capitalized) Named after Orkney, an island off the northern coast of England in the Scottish Isles.

Ossimi: (capitalized) The breed is from Egypt and the name comes from a village near Cairo.

Oxford: (capitalized) Originated in Oxford County, England, where it got its name.

pagliarola: (not capitalized) Breed comes from Italy, but I wasn't able to find anything on the name's origin.

pelibüey: (not capitalized) Originally from Africa, but now raised primarily in South America, Cuba, and Mexico.

Perendale: (capitalized) Developed in New Zealand by G. Perren at Massey University.

pinzirita: (not capitalized) The breed is from Sicily and is derived from the Sicilian word *pinzuni*.

Pitt Island: (capitalized) From New Zealand and named after Pitt Island.

poll merino: (not capitalized) Developed in Australia.

polwarth: (not capitalized) Developed in Australia.

polypay: (not capitalized) Developed in the United States. The name comes from the developers and refers to the payoff they anticipated from this new breed.

Pomeranian coarsewool: (partially capitalized) From the Pomerania region of Germany.

Portland: (capitalized) The breed takes its name from the Isle of Portland off the coast of England.

Priangan: (capitalized) The breed takes its name from the Priangan mountainous region of Indonesia.

rabo largo: (not capitalized) From Brazil. The name comes from Brazilian and means "broad tail."

racka: (not capitalized) The breed has been raised in Hungary for hundreds of years.

Rambouillet: (capitalized) The breed came from the Spanish merino and began in France on the Rambouillet estate about fifty miles south of Paris.

Rasa Aragonesa: (capitalized) The breed originated in

Spain (the Pyrenees) and was named after the Aragonese the people of the region of Aragon.

Red Engadine: (capitalized) The breed is from Switzerland and got its name from where it originated—the Lower Engadin Valley.

Rhoenschaf: (capitalized) From Germany, and the name comes from the mountain where it originated. The sheep are also known as the *Rhon*.

Rideau Arcott: (capitalized) The breed was developed at a Canadian lab. The latter half of its name is an acronym for the Animal Research Centre in Ottawa. The first part of the name may be from one of the researchers as it is a fairly common name in Ottawa. Regardless, since it precedes the proper noun, it is (capitalized)

Romanov: (capitalized) Breed is from Russia and got its name from the town of Romanov.

Romney: (capitalized) Bred in England where the breed took its name from the Romney Marsh region.

rouge de l'quest: (not capitalized) From France. The name translates to "red of the west."

rough fell: not capitalized . From England, and the name derives from the nearby fells (high, barren landscapes).

royal white: (not capitalized) Developed in the United States.

rya: (not capitalized) The breed originated in Sweden. I could find no reference to its naming. By the way, if I could find no reference to a name's origin, I did as I suggested earlier, and left it lowercase. When you have a capitalization question you can't answer, you're better off leaving it lowercase.

ryeland: (not capitalized) Originated in England and got its name from the rye grass it grazed on.

rygja: (not capitalized) From Norway.

Sahel-type: (capitalized) From the Sahel region of Africa.

Santa Cruz: (capitalized) The origin of the sheep are in question, but there is no question regarding the name: they were named after Santa Cruz Island.

Santa Inês: (capitalized) Named for Santa Inés in Brazil.

Sardinian: (capitalized) Named for Sardinia.

Sar Planina: (capitalized) Breed comes from Macedonia and Albania, and the name derives from the Macedonian word for the *Sar Mountains*, hence the capitalization.

Scottish blackface: (partially capitalized) From Scotland.

Sicilian Barbary: (capitalized) From Sicily, and its name comes from its cross with the Tunisian Barbary breed (Barbary Coast).

Shetland: (capitalized) From Scotland, the Shetland Islands.

Shropshire: (capitalized) From Shropshire county in England.

skudde: (not capitalized) The breed comes from Central and Eastern Europe.

Soay: (capitalized) From Scotland, and the name is derived from the island of Soay, off Scotland's coast.

Somali: (capitalized) From Somalia.

Sopravissana: (capitalized) From Italy, and, the name derives from the area of origin, the *comune of Visso*.

South African merino: (partially capitalized) From South Africa.

South African mutton merino: (partially capitalized) From South Africa.

South Suffolk: (capitalized) Originated in England from the Suffolk area.

Southdown: (capitalized) From England, and the name comes from the large numbers of this breed around the South Downs region.

South Wales mountain: (partially capitalized) From South Wales in the mountainous region.

spælsau: (not capitalized) From Norway.

spiegel: (not capitalized) From Germany.

St. Croix (Virgin Island White): (capitalized) Named after the island of St. Croix.

Steigar: (capitalized) Comes from the Steigen region of northern Norway.

steinschaf: (not capitalized) From Germany. The origin of the name is not known.

strong-wool **merino:** (not capitalized) From Australia.

Suffolk: (capitalized) From the Suffolk area of England.

Sumavska: (capitalized) From the Czech and German regions, and the name comes from Sumava Mountain region.

Swaledale: (capitalized) Originated in Northern England and got its name from the dale of the Swale River.

Swedish fur sheep: (partially capitalized) From Sweden.

Targhee: (capitalized) The breed originated in New Zealand and was imported by the United States. It gets its name from the Targhee National Forest in the Northwest.

Teeswater: (capitalized) From England. The Teeswater is found in Northern England, especially Teesdale, County Durham.

Texel: (capitalized) The breed originated on the Isle of Texel, off the coast of the Netherlands.

Thalli: (capitalized) The breed is named after the Thal region of Pakistan.

tong: (not capitalized) From China.

touabire: (not capitalized) From Africa.

tsurcana: (not capitalized) From Romania.

Tunis: (capitalized) Bred in the United States, but the breed got its name from Tunisia.

Tyrol mountain: (partially capitalized) From Austria and the Tyrol Mountains region.

Uda: (capitalized) From Nigeria and named after the Uda people.

Ujumqin: (capitalized) From Mongolia and named after the Ujumqin people of Inner Mongolia.

Ushant: (capitalized) From the island of Ushant off the coast of France.

Valais blacknose: (partially capitalized) From the Valais region of Switzerland.

Vendéen: (capitalized) The Vendéen were developed near Vendée in western France.

walachenschaf: (not capitalized) From Romania. The name probably derives from Wallachia, but I wasn't able to confirm this.

Wallis Country sheep: (partially capitalized) From Upper Wallis in Switzerland.

Waziri: (capitalized) The breed is found in the Waziristan area and Bannu district in NWF Province in Pakistan.

weisse hornlose heidschnucke: (not capitalized) From Germany.

Welsh hill speckled face: (partially capitalized) From Wales and a cross between the Welsh mountain sheep and the Kerry hill sheep.

Welsh mountain: (partially capitalized) From the mountainous regions of Wales.

Welsh mountain badger faced: (partially capitalized) From the mountainous regions of Wales.

Wensleydale: (capitalized) From England. The breed takes its name from Wensleydale, which is the dale or upper valley of the River Ure in North Yorkshire, England. The dale takes its name from the village of Wensley.

West African dwarf: (partially capitalized) From West Africa.

White Suffolk: (capitalized) Named after Suffolk County, in England.

Whiteface Dartmoor: (capitalized) Originated in the Dartmoor region of England.

Whiteface Woodland: (capitalized) The breed takes its name from the Woodlands of Hope, an area in the South Pennines in England.

Wiltshire horn: (partially capitalized) Originated in Wiltshire, in England.

Xinjiang finewool: (partially capitalized) Developed in China and likely named after the Xinjiang region.

*T*he list of recognized sheep breeds contains more Than two hundred names, however, that is by no means a comprehensive list. To give an example, I've listed just the Italian breeds of sheep below. There are ninety-seven of them alone.

And please note that the Italian listing of breeds is not capitalized as it should be. Not all of them should be upper case.

Italian Breeds of Sheep

Alpagota

Altamurana

Appenninica

Bagnolese

Barbaresca

Barisciano, or Aquilana (Abruzzo)

Bellunese (Veneto)

Bergamasca

Biellese

Borgotarese (Emilia-Romagna)

Brentegana

Brianzola

Brigasca

Brogna

Cadorina (Veneto)

Campidano, or Cagliari Sardegna

Carapellese, or Gentile moretta, Gentile a vello nero, Merino nera, Moretta

Carnica (Friuli-Venezia Giulia)

Casciana (Tuscany)

Casentinese (Tuscany)

Chersolina

Chianina, or Val di Chiana (Tuscany)

Chietina (Lazio)

Ciavenasca

Cinta (Lombardy)

Ciuta

Comisana

Cornella Bianca

Cornetta (Emilia-Romagna)

Cornigliese

Corteno

Della Roccia or Steinschaf, Pecora delle rocce, Pecora dei sassi, Carinthia, Tirolese (Trentino-Alto Adige)

Delle Langhe
Di montagna
Fabrianese
Fasanese
Fiemmese, or Val di Fiemme (Trentino-Alto Adige)
Finarda
Frabosana
Friulana, or Furlana (Friuli-Venezia Giulia)
Garessina
Garfagnina Bianca
Gentile di Calabria, or Migliorata di Calabria (Calabria)
Gentile di Lucania, or Migliorata di Lucania (Basilicata)
Gentile di Puglia
Giupanna, or Ragusa-Sipan (Sicily)
Istriana (Carsolina)
Lamon
Laticauda
Leccese
Livo
Maremmana, or Bastarda maremmana, Bastarda spagnola
(Tuscany, Lazio)
Marrana
Massese
Matesina
Merinizzata Italiana
Modenese
Nera di Arbus
Nostrana
Noticiana
Noventana, Monselesana, Pecora di Monselice
Padovana (Veneto)
Pagliarola

Pecora del Jura

Perugina di pianura (Umbria)

Pinzirita

Plezzana

Pomarancina

Pusterese

Quadrella

Reggiana (Emilia-Romagna)

Rosset

Saltasassi

Sambucana

Sampeyrina

Sarda

Savoiarda

Schnalserschaf

Schwarzbraunes Bergschaf

Sciara

Senese, or Senese delle Crete (Tuscany)

Sopravissana

Tacola

Tarina

Tiroler Bergschaf

Trimeticcia Segezia

Turchessa

Urbascia

Val Badia, Badiota (Trentino-Alto Adige)

Valle del Belice

Varesina

Varzese

Vicentina

Villnösser Schaf

Vissana

Zerasca

Zucca Modenese

This list should cover any occurrence you run into regarding capitalization, however, if you need to cite a breed that's not listed, simply follow the rules (after checking your dictionary):

- Capitalize the portion of the name that is derived from a proper noun.
- Capitalize any word preceding that word.
- Do not capitalize words that follow it unless they are proper nouns.

Chapter Twenty-Six

SWINE BREEDS

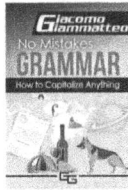

With more than one billion pigs roaming the earth, they constitute one of the largest groups of large mammals on the planet. They are also one of the older domesticated species.

Many people don't even know the breed names, let alone the correct way to capitalize them, so if you have an interest, the following list shows how.

American landrace: (partially capitalized) From America.

American Yorkshire: (capitalized) From America, and the name also derives from Yorkshire.

Angeln saddleback: (partially capitalized) The breed originated in Angeln, Germany by crossing a German landrace with a Wessex saddleback.

Arapawa Island: (capitalized) The Arapawa is a feral breed of pig found on the Arapawa Island off New Zealand.

ba xuyen: (not capitalized) From Vietnam, by the Mekong Delta.

Bantu: (capitalized) From Africa. The name likely derives from the Bantu people.

Basque: (capitalized) From the Basque region of the mountains between France and Spain (the Pyrenees).

bazna: (not capitalized) From Romania.

Beijing black: (partially capitalized) From China and named after Beijing.

Belarus black pied: (partially capitalized) From Belarus, Russia.

Belgian landrace: (partially capitalized) From Belgium.

Bentheim black pied pig: (partially capitalized) Breed originated in Bentheim, Germany.

Berkshire: (capitalized) Originated in the English county of Berkshire.

Black Slavonian: (capitalized) From the heavily forested areas of Slavonia.

Black Iberian pig: (partially capitalized) From the Iberian Peninsula.

Breitovo: (capitalized) From the Breytovo region in Russia.

British landrace: (partially capitalized) From England.

British lop: (partially capitalized) From England and named *lop* because of its long ears.

British saddleback: (partially capitalized) From England and bred with saddleback stock.

Bulgarian white: (partially capitalized) From Bulgaria.

Cantonese: (capitalized) From China.

Celtic pig: (partially capitalized) From Spain and named after the Celtic people.

Chato Murciano: (capitalized) From the Murcia region of Spain.

Chester white: (partially capitalized) From Chester

County, PA., in the United States. Many of the dictionaries I checked with had this capitalized, though I don't know why. Context alone should be enough to clarify things.

Choctaw hog: (partially capitalized) From the United States and named after the Choctaw Indians.

creole pig: (not capitalized) Native to Haiti.

Czech improved white: (partially capitalized) From the Czech Republic.

Danish landrace: (partially capitalized) From Denmark.

duroc: (not capitalized) From the United States.

Dutch landrace: (partially capitalized) From the Netherlands.

Essex: (capitalized) From the Essex region of England.

Estonian bacon: (partially capitalized) From Estonia.

Fengjing: (capitalized) From the Fengjing region of China, near Shanghai.

Finnish landrace: (partially capitalized) From Finland.

forest mountain pig: (not capitalized) Rare breed of pig from Armenia.

French landrace: (partially capitalized) From France.

Gascon: (capitalized) From the Gascony region of France.

German landrace: (partially capitalized) From Germany.

Gloucestershire old spots: (partially capitalized) From England, by Gloucesterhire.

Göttingen minipig: (partially capitalized) From Germany and named after the University of Göttingen, where the breed began.

Guinea hog: (partially capitalized) Bred in the United States. The Guinea hog likely gets its name from the stock coming from Guinea, Africa. That hasn't been confirmed, but it's likely.

Hampshire: (capitalized) From England, in the Hampshire region.

Hereford: (capitalized) From the United States, but named due to the coloring resembling the Hereford cattle, which were named for the Herefordshire region in England.

Hezuo: (capitalized) Named after the Hezuo region of Tibet where the pigs originated.

Iberian: (capitalized) See "Black Iberian pig."

Italian landrace: (partially capitalized) From Italy.

Japanese landrace: (partially capitalized) From Japan.

Jeju black pig: (partially capitalized) From Jejudo Island off Korea.

Jinhua: (capitalized) From the Jinhua region of China.

Kakhetian pig: (partially capitalized) From the Kakheti region of Georgia.

Kele: (capitalized) From China, near the Kele region of Guizhou.

Korean native pig: (partially capitalized) Indigenous to Korea.

krskopolje: (not capitalized) From Slovenia.

kunekune: (not capitalized) From New Zealand, and *kunekune* is a Maori word meaning "fat and round."

Lacombe: (capitalized) From Canada and named for the Lacombe Research Center in Lacombe, Alberta.

large black: (not capitalized) From England.

large black-white: (not capitalized) From England.

large white: (not capitalized) From England.

Latvian white: (partially capitalized) From Latvia.

Lithuanian native: (partially capitalized) From Lithuania.

Lithuanian white: (partially capitalized) From Lithuania.

mangalitza: (not capitalized) From Hungary.

Meishan: (capitalized) From the Meishan region of China.

middle white: (not capitalized) From England.

minzhu: (not capitalized) From China, and the name translates roughly to "folk pig."

Mong Cai: (capitalized) From Vietnam and named after the Mong Cai region.

Mora Romagnola: (capitalized) From the Emilia-Romagna region of Italy.

Mukota: (capitalized) Named after the Mukota region of Zimbabwe.

mulefoot: (not capitalized) From Spain. The name comes from the pig's hooves which are said to resemble a mule's.

myrhorod pig: (not capitalized) From the Ukraine.

Nero Siciliano: (capitalized) From Sicily.

Neijiang: (capitalized) From China and named after Neijiang city.

Ningxiang: (capitalized) From the Ningxiang region of the Hunan province in China.

Norwegian landrace: (partially capitalized) From Norway.

Ossabaw Island: (capitalized) Named after Ossabaw Island, Georgia. They were put on the island originally by Spanish soldiers as a food source but have been feral for hundreds of years.

Oxford sandy and black: (partially capitalized) From the Oxfordshire region of England.

Philippine native: (partially capitalized) From the Philippines.

Pietrain: (capitalized) Native to Belgium, the breed takes its name from the village of Piétrain.

Poland China: (capitalized) From the United States and named after the initial breeding attempts using pigs from Poland and China.

red wattle: (not capitalized) From the United States and named for its coloring and the distinctive wattle.

saddleback: (not capitalized)

Siberian black pied. (partially capitalized) From Siberia.

spots: (not capitalized) From England.

Swedish landrace: (partially capitalized) From Sweden.

swallow-bellied **mangalitza:** (not capitalized) From Hungary.

Taihu pig: (partially capitalized) Named after the Lake Tai region by the Yellow River in China.

Tamworth: (capitalized) From the Tamworth region of England.

thuoc nhieu: (not capitalized) From Vietnam.

Tibetan: (capitalized) From Tibet.

Turopolje: (capitalized) Named for Turopolje, Croatia, where the breed originates.

Ukranian white steppe: (partially capitalized) From the Ukraine.

Ukrainian spotted steppe: (partially capitalized) From the Ukraine.

Vietnamese potbelly: (partially capitalized) From Vietnam.

Welsh: (capitalized) Named for Wales.

Wessex saddleback: (partially capitalized) From the Wessex region of England.

Wuzhishan: (capitalized) From the Wuzishan district of China.

Yorkshire: (capitalized) From the Yorkshire region of England.

Chapter Twenty-Seven

UNTITLED BREEDS AND OTHER ITEMS

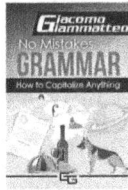

The preceding chapters on capitalization covered a lot, but not nearly all there is to address. We didn't touch on fish, plants, trees, and many more.

But that would be difficult, much like covering the wine varietals would be. There are more than twenty thousand species of fish alone, each with a unique scientific and common name.

Now is not the time for frustration though. If you follow the rules we established, you shouldn't have any problem. Let's look at a few:

- African cichlid
- auratus
- banded cichlid
- bass
- bumblebee cichlid
- snakehead
- South American mouthbrooder

- swordfish
- Texas cichlid
- tuna

As you can see, the names that are capitalized are the ones containing a proper noun.

The United States Fish and Wildlife Service is a lot like the AKC or the Cat Fanciers; they would have you capitalize far too much, but if you stick to the rules you should be fine.

Plants and trees bring a new issue to light; they are often referred to by their Latin name, and there are separate capitalization rules regarding the listing of genus, species, etc.

In short, you always capitalize the first letter of the genus, but keep the species name lowercased, however, both genus and species are placed in italics. The common name is lowercased unless it is a proper noun or derives from a proper noun. I'm not going to go into a lot of detail with this, but I'll cite a few examples.

Suppose you're writing about the "pin oak," and you want to make sure to get your capitalization straight.

- First, identify the genus: *Quercus.*
- Second, the species: *palustris.*
- Third, the common name: *pin oak.*

You might write:

Quercus palustris, the "pin oak" or "swamp oak," is native to many parts of the Northeast and is found as far west as Oklahoma and Kansas.

Pinus palustris, the Georgia pine (also known as the longleaf pine) is widespread in the southeastern part of the country.

For all of these items, it's best to look it up in the dictionary first. If it's not listed, resort to doing an internet search or searching on Wikipedia.

By the way, the rules cited for capitalization of genus and species apply to all items, not just plants. So if referring to any of the following by their scientific names, the capitalization seen below would apply.

- *Canis lupus*, gray wolf or timber wolf
- *Tursiops truncatus, bottlenose dolphin*
- *Ursus maritimus, polar bear*

But if the common name has a proper noun in it or is derived from a proper noun, it is capitalized.

- *Ursus arctos middendorffi,* Kodiak bear or Alaskan brown bear

No matter which name you refer to the animal as, it would be capitalized. *Kodiak* is derived from Kodiak Island off the coast of Alaska, and of course, *Alaska* comes from the name of the state. This is the same as the following example:

- *Dissostichus eleginoides,* Chilean sea bass

That sums it up. Armed with these few rules and a good dictionary, you should be able to correctly capitalize anything.

Chapter Two

SUMMARY

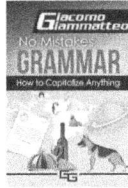

If you've suffered through any significant part of this, you now realize the complexities of capitalization (and the importance of getting it right).

Some words need capitalization and a lot of them are not recorded as entries in dictionaries or covered in style guides. Do your best to follow the rules, but if a question arises, and if you can't find a trusted resource to verify the proper way to capitalize, then use your best judgment to make a decision, and regardless of your decision, be consistent.

ACKNOWLEDGMENTS

It is with great honor that I give eternal gratitude to my wife and all four of my grandkids. They give me the inspiration to keep going.

I also need to thank my editor, Michele Preisendorf, of Eschler Editing, for her undying patience and diligence in keeping me straight.

ABOUT THE AUTHOR

Giacomo Giammatteo is the author of gritty crime dramas about murder, mystery, and family. He also writes non-fiction books including the No Mistakes Careers series, No Mistakes Publishing, No Mistakes Grammar, and No Mistakes Writing.

When Giacomo isn't writing, he's helping his wife take care of the animals on their sanctuary. At last count, they had forty-five animals—eleven dogs, a horse, six cats, and twenty-six pigs.

Oh, and one crazy—and very large—wild boar, who takes walks with Giacomo every day and also happens to be his best buddy.

nomistakespublishing.com
gg@giacomog.com

ALSO BY GIACOMO GIAMMATTEO

You can see all of my books here.

And you can buy them on the platform of your choice.

This brings up a thought: with more than fifty books out now, it is becoming difficult to try to update the list in the back of all of them. If you want to know what books I have out, use the link above, which takes you to my website, or download the latest copy of my GG recommended reading list, which is free.

Nonfiction :

Careers:

No Mistakes Resumes, Book I of No Mistakes Careers

No Mistakes Interviews, Book II of No Mistakes Careers

Grammar:

Misused Words, No Mistakes Grammar, Volume I

Misused Words for Business, No Mistakes Grammar, Volume II

More Misused Words, No Mistakes Grammar, Volume III

Visual Grammar (this is a compilation of volumes I–III with a bit of new information added. It also includes pictures. The world's first visual grammar book)

Racing Sayings"

No Mistakes Grammar Bites Volume XVI, "Which and What" and "Since and Because"

No Mistakes Grammar Bites Volume XVII, "Hyphens, and When to Use Them" and "Em Dashes and En Dashes"

No Mistakes Grammar Bites Volume XVIII, "Words Difficult to Pronounce" and "Could Not Care Less"

No Mistakes Grammar Bites Volume XIX, "Punctuation" and "When You Don't Need the Word Personal"

No Mistakes Grammar Bites, Volume XX, "When Is Currently Needed?" And "Intervene and Interfere"

No Mistakes Grammar Bites, Volume XXI, "More Hyphen Questions" and Myself, Me, Themselves and Themselves."

No Mistakes Grammar Bites, Volume XXII, "Words You May Be Using Wrong, Part One"

No Mistakes Grammar Bites, Volume XXIII, Words You May Be Using Wong, Part II

No Mistakes Grammar Bites, Volume XXIV, "If and Whether," and "Incredible"

No Mistakes Grammar Bites, Volume XXV, "Use or Utilize" and "Dilemma"

No Mistakes Grammar Bites, Volume XXVI, "Alternate and Alternative" and "Plethora"

Writing:

No Mistakes Writing, Volume I—Writing Shortcuts

No Mistakes Writing, Volume II—How to Write a Bestseller

No Mistakes Writing, Volume III—Editing Made Easy

No Mistakes Writing, Volume IV—Writing Rules for Writers Who Don't Like Rules (coming soon)

Publishing:

How to Publish an eBook, No Mistakes Publishing, Volume I

How to Format an eBook, No Mistakes Publishing, Volume II

eBook Distribution, No Mistakes Publishing, Volume III

Print on Demand—Who to Use to Print Your Books, No Mistakes Publishing, Volume IV

Other nonfiction

Uneducated

Whiskers and Bear—Volume I, Sanctuary Tales

A Collection of Animal Stories, Volume II, Sanctuary Tales

More Animal Stories, Volume III, Sanctuary Tales Surviving a Stroke —or Two

Life and Then Some

Fiction:

Friendship & Honor Series:

Murder Takes Time

Murder Has Consequences

Murder Takes Patience

Murder Is Invisible

Murder Is a Promise

Murder Is Immaculate (coming soon)

Blood Flows South Series:

A Bullet For Carlos: A Connie Gianelli Mystery

Finding Family, a Novella

A Bullet From Dominic

The Good Book

The Ranger (coming soon)

Redemption Series:

Necessary Decisions: A Gino Cataldi Mystery

Old Wounds

Promises Kept, the Story of Number Two

Premeditated

The Ranger (coming soon)

Rules of Vengeance Series: (Fantasy)

Light of Lights (the beginning, a novella)

A Promise of Vengeance

Undeniable Vengeance

Consummate Vengeance

Vengeance Is Mine (2019)

Note. The Light of Lights is a novella. It's about 100 pages long and sets the stage for the series. The other books in the series are between 650 and 850 pages long.

∾

OTHER BOOKS

You can always see the current and coming-soon books on my website.

Fiction:

Memories for Sale (mystery/sf)

The Joshua Citadel (SF novella)

Children's Books:

No Mistakes Grammar for Kids, Volume I—Much and Many

No Mistakes Grammar for Kids, Volume II—Lie and Lay

*No Mistakes Grammar for Kids, Volume III—*Bring and Take

No Mistakes Grammar for Kids, Volume IV, "Would've, Should've" and "Your and You're"

No Mistakes Grammar for Kids, Volume V, "There, They're, and Their" and "To, Too, and Two"

Shinobi Goes to School—Life on the Farm for Kids, Volume I

Fiona Gets Caught, Life on the Farm for Kids, Volume II

Coco Gets a Donut, Life on the Farm for Kids, Volume III

Squeak Gets a Home, Life on the Farm for Kids, Volume IV

Biscotti Saves Punch, Life on the Farm for Kids, Volume V

The Adventures of Adalina, Volume I, Adalina and the Five Tiny Bears

Coming Soon:

The Adventures of Adalina, Volume II, Adalina and the Underwater Bears

Get on the mailing list, and you'll be sure to be notified of release dates and sales.

Mailing list

And don't forget to leave a review!

www.ingramcontent.com/pod-product-compliance
Lightning Source LLC
Chambersburg PA
CBHW050225270326
41914CB00003BA/569